The Collector's Mother

The Collector's Mother

How an Underprivileged Woman Inspired Her Son to Become an IAS Officer

Bishnupada Sethi

ink | OCCAM

ISBN: 978-81-968471-8-0

First published in India 2024
This edition published 2024

BluOne Ink Pvt. Ltd
A-76, 2nd Floor, Sector 136, Noida
Uttar Pradesh 201301
www.bluone.ink
publisher@bluone.ink

Printed and bound in India at Nutech Print Services -India

Kali, Occam and BluPrint are all trademarks of BluOne Ink Pvt. Ltd.

ink | OCCAM

To my daughter, Mahima, and son, Alekh, who have inherited values and grit from their grandparents

Contents

1

Passage to Immortality

When things are going well in our lives, we often tend not to pay much attention to the events happening around us. Our everyday emotions and activities do not tend to leave a significant impact on our minds, so we do not usually reflect on them. However, when we face an unusual and life-shattering event, we pause to cope with the emerging situation first. While we regain our bearings, we tend to analyse the situation, hoping to find reasons, connections, causes, effects, and hidden truths. Sometimes, we even go beyond rationality in our quest for understanding.

One of the greatest dilemmas we face in life is when someone we love passes away. The sudden departure of a loved one can leave us feeling miserable and we wonder if something could have been done to prevent it. We often reflect on the departed person's entire life and our relationship with them, and become perplexed with questions such as life after death, the transmigration of the soul, connections beyond earthly existence, and the purpose of life.

Everyone has to face death eventually, as it is an inevitable part of life. It is believed that the dance of death happens continuously around us, but we often fail to notice it. However, when it comes to our loved ones, we tend to probe deeper into the events leading to their death to understand if warning signs were given or their life had meaning. It is only through our close association with such individuals that we are prompted to reflect on these matters. Many religious, spiritual, and philosophical explanations exist in this vast cosmos, which guide our daily lives. Our beliefs are often shaped by the culture and society we grew up in and different religions have their own unique interpretations of life and death. Despite being indoctrinated from a young age, we often turn to these beliefs to find solace during times of tragedy. As an avid reader, I have been influenced by books such as *Dying to Be Me* by Anita Moorjani, *Many Lives Many Masters* by Dr Brian Weiss, *Spirits I Have Known* by Ishita Roy Chakraverti, and many others. These authors emphasize the idea that we are all ageless travellers and that our journey does not end with our deaths. I tend to believe that there is more to life than what we can see with our eyes or feel with our senses. We all have a vast past and future, but only a short present. It may be difficult to explain why we cannot remember our earthly existence in the mother's womb, despite being there. Like many others, I have always been curious and reflective. Over time, I have come to believe that there is a strong relationship between the causes and effects of our real-life experiences.

As mortals, we can only vividly remember certain parts of our journey, while most experiences inevitably fade from our memory over time. The path we take is rarely linear and often filled with difficulties and challenging times. Dreams and despair play a game of hide and seek with us, making our journey both easy and challenging. At times, we may wonder why we are on this journey at all. Is it similar to the planets and celestial bodies, which must have started at some point in space and time? As we near the end of our journey, our strength wears out, and the road ahead tapers out. Only when we develop our consciousness, do we begin to know people and, before that, no one was known. Many people join us at various points in our lives, identified by names and some claiming to be related to us. While some may leave us in the middle of the journey, others will stay with us until the end. The process of joining and leaving us continues throughout. However, despite all the people around us, our inner self makes us feel that we are a lonely being and that we carry our own baggage. No one is with us, and no one will accompany us on our journey for all time or forever.

My native village is located in the district of Balasore in Odisha, which is on the border with West Bengal. It takes about 5 hours to drive down from Bhubaneswar. I visit my home frequently for various reasons, but the foremost reason is to be with my parents, who have lived there for most of their entire life. Recently, the villagers requested that I visit the village for a festive occasion. I reached there on 5 March 2022 wishing to see my parents and attend a puja in the village the next day. Ever since I left my village as a child to pursue my studies and later for a job, I have always made it a point to visit my parents regularly so they remain in good health and spirits. Over time, some of the villagers have approached me for assistance with various matters such as medical emergencies, case matters, admission to educational institutions, bank loans, benefits under various schemes of the government, getting infrastructure like road, water, electricity, school building, and even the posting of teachers to the area.

When I visited my home, my mother would always greet me warmly and lead me to our house. She took great care in ensuring I was comfortable and that my room was clean and ready for my exclusive use. All my belongings would be neatly stored in a trunk, and as soon as I arrived, she would ensure that food and water were served. However, during my last visit, I noticed a significant change in her behaviour. She asked me to take her to the hospital in Bhubaneswar in an unusual manner and she did not allow me to stay in the village for even one day, even though a puja and village feast was scheduled the following day. Although she seemed weak and pale, it appeared like she was more uncertain about something rather than very unwell. She had been visiting a doctor at the nearby government dispensary whenever she felt ill.

During my latest visit, I noticed a significant change in the way she interacted with me. Rather than making a simple request, it seemed like she was giving me instructions. Her behaviour lacked the usual warmth, and she did not ask me if I needed anything to make myself comfortable. She rushed me through unpacking and eating as if a deep fear was driving her. Although she did not show it outwardly, I could sense her unease.

I made it a habit to talk to my mother at least twice a day, once in the morning and once in the evening, to check on her well-being and that of my father. This had been my routine for several years since I moved away from the village. I was aware that due to her advanced age, my mother's health had not been at its best for some time. In the past, whenever she was unwell, we brought her to an excellent private hospital in Bhubaneswar for treatment. She would return to the village when she fully recovered and became medically fit. She was usually hospitalized in Bhubaneswar twice a year for less than a week each time. There have been occasions when her condition had become severe, and she needed to be put on a ventilator and kept in the ICU, but with good care and treatment by the doctors, she always recovered. However, during the COVID-19 pandemic, we could not bring her to Bhubaneswar for treatment when she needed hospitalization to avoid infection. Compared to urban areas, only a few people were getting infected due to COVID-19 or dying in the village. The crisis was of a great magnitude in the city. During the pandemic, she received local treatment and fortunately recovered.

I sensed her urgency and quickly contacted my friend who works at the hospital to arrange her admission upon arrival. We started our journey back to Bhubaneswar within half an hour. I noticed how hurriedly my mother gathered the few things she needed in the hospital and how she burst into tears as we got into the car. This was unlike her usual happy self, so I knew something was wrong. As we began our journey, she gradually became more comfortable, and we talked about many important events in our lives. Upon reaching Bhubaneswar, I wasted no time admitting her to the city hospital that evening. She was kept under observation for the first night, but thankfully did not require much attention from the doctor.

From 5 March to 8 March , she underwent several tests in the hospital. She was administered medication that she had been taking for several months. The doctor said her condition was good and did not require prolonged hospitalization. They advised that she stay away from the hospital environment for better recovery. The treating doctor and nursing staff were all familiar with her and treated her in a friendly and warm manner. She conversed with them fondly and recalled her previous visits to the hospital. She appeared very informal and pleasant with them.

However, I noticed something unusual in her behaviour this time. At times, she seemed disconnected from the current conversation and would start talking about unrelated topics. For example, she began to mistake her current doctor, who had been treating her for eight years, for a physician she knew in her childhood days, over seventy years prior. She would tell tales of how, in her ancestral village, the old doctor would travel around treating patients and how he kept a young girl to cook for him since he had no one else. The old doctor resembled her current doctor, who was also very kind-hearted. I would try to bring her back to the present and remind her that her current doctor was a young man whom she knew well, but she would continue to talk about people, places, and times we did not know.

When I asked, the doctor simply said it was due to temporary loss of memory, a symptom of old age, and nothing to worry about. Before she was taken to the hospital, I knew about her involvement in various activities in the village. For the past few years, she had been performing the worship of Goddess Basanti at our village home. She had made a vow before the goddess for my well-being, and in her prayer, she promised to perform the puja of the goddess in our home once I grew up and became worthy of something. To fulfil this vow, village artisans made idols, and the priest performed the puja. Every year, a feast would be arranged for relatives, guests, and villagers. This year, she made preliminary arrangements for the puja. Unfortunately, she had to be hospitalized.

During her first night in the hospital, she had a lengthy conversation with my elder sister, who lives in the village. They discussed several essential things related to my mother's daily life. Suddenly, she informed my sister that the puja would not take place this year. During the pandemic, the government prohibited all public activities, including puja, and my mother had abided by this rule. However, since the government lifted the restrictions this year, we felt that she could be telling these things due to her memory problems, as her doctor had previously stated. At first, we did not take her comments seriously, but they became increasingly bizarre and stuck in our minds. During her hospitalization, the treatment provided was simple. The doctor had been giving her conservative treatment for several years, as major interventions like surgery were not possible due to her old age. She was mostly kept under observation and provided with the usual medication. On 8 March, she was discharged from the hospital. She stayed in Bhubaneswar until 11 March to receive the best possible post-hospitalization care. The doctor advised against sending her back to the village immediately and cautioned them to avoid the long road journey for her complete recovery.

However, from 9 March morning onwards, my mother began expressing irritation and impatience. She cried and complained as if she were being held captive and demanded to be sent to the village without further delay. I tried to persuade her to stay a few more days, but she remained steadfast. During our travels, she always carried her holy scriptures and would read from them in the morning and evening. One evening, while I was seated beside her, she read a chapter from the Mahabharata about the Kauravs' unfair killing of Abhimanyu.

One morning over the three days, I went to her room and was surprised by her appearance. Her face was turned away from the sun's rays shining through the glass window, and she appeared solemn and still. Her long hair was unkempt and dishevelled. She was trance-like, not speaking as if she had been sitting in that position for some time. I had to approach her and shake her to bring her out of it.

Sometimes, she would speak out of context and say more than usual. I did not mind much about this behaviour. However, one day, I noticed she looked at me sternly, something she had never done before. She was always soft and caring towards me. Even when she knew I had made mistakes and shortcomings, she would never tell me because she did not want to hurt me. But this time, she scolded me for having a spotless house and advised me not to stray from it. She said the home was a place of peace and virtue, and her message was quite cryptic. While speaking, she seemed emotionless, like a wise monk, as if she knew everything about me and the situations I might face. Her advice was impartial and dispassionate.

I want to share that I have survived very adverse situations in life. My mother played a significant role in my life as my guardian angel. She was always overprotective of me since I was a child. She did everything she could to take care of me, keep me happy, and inspire me to achieve great things. She never scolded or punished me; instead, she would step in front of me to protect me from any adversity. I learned a lot from her silence, and she always guided me in the right direction.

Hence, I was surprised by her rude behaviour and could not understand why she was reprimanding me for no apparent reason. However, I did not argue with her as usual and did not ask for any further explanation. She wanted to go to the village as soon as possible, so I arranged a comfortable journey on 11 March with a proper escort.

The previous evening, my mother spent time with my daughter. She read from the Mahabharata and expressed happiness in my daughter's company. She had lost her appetite, but she had a little breakfast after some persuasion. As she was leaving, I took a few photographs with her. Usually, as a mark of respect, I would ask for her blessings by touching her feet whenever she left Bhubaneswar for the village. However, this time, I felt a little hesitant to do so. Instead, I prostrated before her like we often do before a goddess to seek blessings. This I had never done before.

While I was accompanying her to the car, holding her hand, I suggested I come to see her off. While sitting in the car, she said, 'You have come to bid me farewell.' Her tone was firm, and she seemed to be hinting at something. Although her statement took me aback, I did not attach too much importance to it. However, those words remained with me.

She was overjoyed to be back in the village with my father. She resumed her regular activities and restricted her movements due to weakness caused by the hospitalization and long road journey.

To everyone's surprise, she woke up early on 19 March. She walked around the village, visited all the houses she frequented, sat with the villagers, and discussed various topics. The conversations were deep and intimate with people she was fond of. She only returned home by lunchtime. As she had spent several hours walking around the village, her legs had swollen. It was a hot and sultry day.

She complained that the heat was unbearable and she might not survive.

The day before her death, my mother spoke to my father about the usual things. During the conversation, she requested that nobody should take her body to Puri after she passed away. Usually, people from Odisha believe that being cremated at Swargadwar in Puri will help them attain salvation according to Hindu beliefs. She felt that I would insist on performing her last rites in Puri. However, my mother did not want to be cremated in Puri and requested that her last rites be performed in our village instead. She even pointed to a timber tree on our land that could be used to prepare the wood for her cremation. Despite talking about her death, she remained calm and composed throughout the conversation.

After returning to the village from the hospital, my mother took her belongings from the trunk, including new and old sarees, money, and jewellery. She had many new sarees and began to distribute them amongst those she was familiar with over a week. It was an unusual behaviour, and my father believed she was not in the right frame of mind. He locked her belongings in a suitcase and kept the key with him, fearing she might give everything away.

There are several households in the neighbourhood, some of whom are related through blood. Our origin can be traced to a common ancestor who migrated to this village from Bengal about a century and a half ago. According to Hindu customs, all relatives from the paternal side of the family perform rituals for events such as birth, death, marriage, worship, and other occasions in life. For specific reasons to be explained later, our relationship with our neighbours was very bitter. We have faced hostility, jealousy, and aggression from them. They even wished to eliminate us at some point in the past. We have suffered immensely due to their ruthless actions, and it can be said that we have survived only due to the grace of God. We never visited our neighbours' homes or engaged in friendly conversations with them for many years. We also did not participate in their traditional ceremonies or follow the required rituals, and they did the same with us. As a result, we did not have any kinship relations with them. My mother had mentioned several times that we had severed our kinship ties with our neighbours.

However, with time, our relationship with the families in our neighbourhood returned to normal. We came to talking terms and participated in social exchanges like any other villager. However, any kinship relationship during ceremonial occasions was non-existent. As time passed and I joined the civil service, we progressed financially and socially, and our neighbours could no longer harm us. Yet, due to the bitter memories of our previous disputes, my mother refused to fully restore our kinship relationship for many years, even after all practical purposes had been resolved.

For several years, the villagers were divided over petty issues. Some local politicians took advantage and divided the villagers into several small groups. In the distant past, the entire village population would participate in village festivals, weddings, feasts, religious ceremonies, and school functions. However, due to the strained relationships, these events took place in small groups, and people from other groups were not invited. During election times, the villagers would turn against one another, and the atmosphere would become toxic. The environment was extremely unhealthy, to say the least.

Over the past few years, my mother has been very socially active in our small village. Once she was elected as a ward member, she fought for the rights of the poor to help them get enlisted for various benefits from the government. At times, she would seek my assistance to help a needy person. During the COVID-19 pandemic, our villagers faced difficult times as the agriculture sector was severely affected. The export of betel leaf, the major source of income for the villagers, had stopped. At that time, my mother would ask me to send some relief to the village. She would find ways to help the villagers and needy people and seek my involvement in areas such as medical treatment in better hospitals, land matters, and inclusion under the welfare scheme. Her activities kept her happy, involved, and appreciated by everyone in the village.

Over time, she played an active role in her village. She organized several meetings to discuss the state of the dilapidated Shitala and Manasa Devi temples. Thanks to the involvement of the village youth, the temples were restored to their former glory. On ceremonial occasions, she took on the role of inviting people from all different factions. As a result of her efforts, the villagers became united, which is now very much visible.

Recently, she decided to bring together all the members of our neighbourhood to forget past grievances and unite as a community. I was extremely surprised by the decision. I knew her and all the sufferings she had endured. She had faced murderous attacks from her neighbours and had survived only by some miracle. All her miseries had started decades ago when the neighbours became jealous of my parents, forcing them to leave the village and sell everything they had. I will later narrate what happened in the past that she could not forgive anyone for. I often wondered where she got the strength to forget all the sad chapters of her life and forgive her enemies. The only answer she gave me was that all of them should be part of her funeral ceremony after her demise. She did not want to be reminded of the pain she had undergone in the past. She had forgiven all.

In 2022, Holi was celebrated on 19 March. After moving around the village, she returned home around noon feeling uncomfortable due to the high temperature and humidity. Later in the evening, after taking a bath, she felt unwell. She was taken to a nearby community health centre, where she usually goes for minor ailments.

I received the information that she went to the hospital in the evening. The boys who accompanied her informed us that her symptoms were not alarming. She had been in worse conditions before and had overcome more critical health problems in the past. Typically, if advised by the doctor, she would be referred to the Balasore headquarters hospital or transported by vehicle to Bhubaneswar. No lifesaving support was required in this instance. She was familiar with the doctor who usually treated her at the hospital and cared for her like a son. As usual, I was informed over the phone whenever she faced any health issues, and all necessary arrangements would be made at the hospital.

I believed everything was normal, as in the past, and she would have returned as no one had called from the hospital. But after an hour, when I called Jagannath, who had accompanied her to the hospital, he burst into tears and said that although she was fine when she walked from the car to a hospital bed, she breathed her last while the doctor was preparing her for an injection. Finding it difficult to break the news to me, they did not call me.

My mother was the most precious to me on this earth. She sacrificed everything to bring me up and always had prayers on her lips for my welfare. She worshipped all the gods and goddesses in the Hindu tradition to ensure that no harm ever came my way, and she even kept several vows for this purpose. Whenever I faced even the slightest difficulties, she would break down. Despite facing constant adversity throughout her life, she persevered with great mental strength and overcame many critical situations. Happiness was like a mirage to her because she had faced so much hardship.

For over four decades, she endured murderous attacks and numerous humiliations due to land disputes. She faced a prolonged hospitalization following an attack by a wild bull. Despite enduring years of poverty, she worked tirelessly to keep her family afloat. She had to shoulder multiple responsibilities from the tender age of nine when she was married off, sacrificing her youth and entire life for her family.

She was a deeply spiritual person who firmly believed in the theory of karma. Whenever I asked her about the troubles she faced in her life, she would simply reply that everything she experienced was a result of her past actions in previous births. She never missed a day reading from holy scriptures like Mahabharata, *Brahma Vaivarta Purana*, Bhagavad Gita, and many others. Her favourite place to do this was near the Tulsi plant in front of our house, where she would sit and delve into these sacred texts. Since childhood, I enjoyed sitting beside her and listening to the beautiful stories she would tell.

She followed Shri Chaitanya Maha Prabhu and believed in Vaishnavism. She never harmed anyone, even when she was mistreated. Her life was one of high morality. When she was in Bhubaneswar for the last time, she told my elder sister over the phone from her hospital bed that she would be leaving very early in the morning. On 20 March, we cremated her in the wee hours in the presence of hundreds of people who genuinely loved her. She had chosen the cremation site and timber beforehand. It makes me wonder if she had a premonition about the exact time of her passing!

I had carefully listened to her words during the time I spent with her from 5 to 11 March. Additionally, I was informed about her activities up until her last breath. Upon reflecting on her words, expressions, emotions, utterances, and activities, I have noticed something very unusual. I believe that those words were not due to temporary memory loss, as a doctor might like to say, but rather signals from an imminent departure of a divine soul.

From my early days, I knew my mother was not an ordinary woman. She gave me life and raised me with great love and affection. She gave me a sense of direction in life and worked tirelessly to provide me with whatever comfort she could. She was like an angel, always surrounding me with care and support. Our relationship was inseparable. In the end, my mother showed total forgiveness to all those who had tormented her. She let go of all the bitterness she had carried her whole life and brought everyone together through family bonds. She may not have read much about the act of forgiveness by Jesus or any other great soul, yet she left this world after performing a similar act in her way.

2

A Fearful Village Atmosphere

As a child, I used to notice two elderly women living in a small hut in front of the house of Kanaka Das, the most influential person in our village. Their hut was situated by the roadside in a small part of a large area. As a curious child, I wondered how they survived without any male member taking care of them and why people hardly visited their house. When I asked my mother about it, she shared a hair-raising story about the family. However, no one dared to discuss the matter openly out of fear of repercussions from Kanaka Das.

In the 1950s, an important incident occurred in my village. The father of Kanaka Das, Judra, arranged for his daughter Faulati to marry a man from their own caste, Dushwar Datta, who was also from the village. Unfortunately, Dushwar passed away at a young age without leaving any children behind. Dushwar's brother, Kurendra, had his eyes on his brother's land and wanted to deprive Faulati of her share of the property. According to the existing norms of the society, Kurendra would have received Dushwar's share of the property if Faulati had not remarried and stayed in the joint family until her death.

However, Faulati did not have a good relationship with her husband's family, so she had a different plan.

At one point in time, Judra Das had no son to be his legal heir. As it was necessary to have a male legal heir due to the prevailing social customs, he brought his sister's son Netra to live with his family with the intention of adopting him later on. However, when three sons were born to Judra subsequently, there was no need to adopt Netra. Netra was a shy and simple person who was more friendly with women than the men in the village. When Netra became an adult, Judra Das decided to get him married. But no one would give their daughters in marriage to Netra, who had no source of livelihood nor any property. So, Judra created some false documents showing that Netra owned some property. This convinced a man from a nearby village to agree to the marriage of his daughter to Netra. Later, the girl and her parents protested when the truth came to light that Netra was a pauper. However, they could not do anything against Judra, a wealthy man. The girl's family had no option but to accept their fate.

At the same time, there was frequent tension and quarrelling within Faulati's husband's family, particularly between Faulati and her brother-in-law. During these arguments, Faulati often threatened to transfer her share of the family property to Netra, which made Kurendra uneasy. He did not trust his sister-in-law and feared that an outsider would receive a large share of his ancestral property. As a result, Kurendra became jealous of Netra.

During the olden days, there was no modern banking system. Instead, people relied on village money lenders for loans. People used to hoard their wealth through gold ornaments and silver coins. I recall seeing such silver coins in the possession of our villagers during my childhood. Under British rule, silver coins were issued during different phases, such as under the East India Company and by the Imperial authority of the crown. The coins featured portraits of Queen Victoria, Edward VII, George V, and George VI. The wealthy people in the village would often convert their wealth into silver coins and hide them in secret places in the house, cow sheds, or underground. The locations were chosen so that outsiders could not guess where they were. Those were dark times in our country when there was little safety and security for life and property. There was a constant fear of invasion and robbery by outsiders, and theft was common. The police system had not yet appropriately evolved and the borders were porous. Due to a lack of trust, only a few family members would know where secret stashes of hoarded wealth were hidden. It was also believed that if someone left behind wealth in the form of gold and silver coins in a hidden place and died, then all such wealth would be passed on to a demigod named Yaksha. Yaksha would then return the wealth to the same person in their next life. There were stories of people encountering Yaksha, and if someone suddenly became rich, it was attributed to getting wealth from the demigod. Given these factors, it was necessary to hide silver coins underground so that they would not be taken away by anyone else. Faulati had received a large quantity of silver coins from her husband and had kept them in a utensil called '*kui*' in a secret location. The total value of the coins was very high. However, Kurendra knew about the silver coins and had an eye on them. One day, Kurendra did not spot the kui. He was devastated and thought that Faulati must have given all her coins to Netra. He was filled with anger and greed and started looking for a way to teach Netra a lesson.

During that time, a constable in our village held a lot of power. Gailash was responsible for reporting to the local police outpost every day. If desired, he could frame anyone in a false case with the help of the local police. He would take agricultural produce, rice, and other items from the village to keep his officers in a good mood. There were times when the Odisha government restricted the transport of paddy and rice from our state to Bengal due to low production and scarcity. This system greatly benefitted the constable. He would sit near the border and seize goods from people, taking them home for himself. De facto, he was the government in the village. With his large body and loud voice, he could intimidate anyone without needing a firearm, making these qualities essential for his policing job with only a lathi.

Kurendra, a friend of the constable, talked to him about Faulati's behaviour and how she had transferred her wealth to Netra. Gailash believed Kurendra, and they both planned to teach Netra a lesson. According to the plan, one day, around noon, Gailash and his companions were catching fish from a village pond near Gailash's house. Gailash's bother

Gahana, his friend Kurendra, and a Muslim man from the neighbouring Medinipur district joined them. They invited Netra to come to the pond and watch the fishing activity. No one else was present at the location. While Netra was sitting on the embankment and enjoying the scene, someone pushed him into the water. Gailash quickly trapped him under a conical fishing net attached to wooden sticks traditionally called '*khupi*'. Gailash used his full strength to keep him underwater for a few minutes. Netra used his entire might to escape and begged Gailash to release him, even calling him 'father'. However, Gailash and others were unmoved. Finally, Gailash succeeded in drowning Netra. There were people working in betel leaf vines nearby who heard the yelling and loud noises but did not understand what was happening. They thought that Gailash and his companions were making loud noises while trying to catch fish in the pond, which they considered quite normal.

A few hours had passed, and Netra's wife and mother waited for him to return home for lunch. He usually left the house without informing anyone, but he would always return by lunchtime. The village boundary was his limit. As time passed, news of his disappearance spread throughout the village. The other villagers joined Netra's family, searching for him in every nook and corner of the village he frequented. The news of his disappearance spread like wildfire to neighbouring villages and people started looking for him there as well. Nobody thought about the possibility of him being dead. After killing Netra, Gailash and his accomplices hid the body under a log of wood in the pond. In the middle of the night, both brothers quietly retrieved the body from the pond and dropped it in another pond located behind Judra Das's house. Gailash chose Netra's uncle's pond to confuse the villagers.

The next day, when the women of Judra Das's household went to the pond early in the morning, they were aghast to see Netra's body floating near the pond's embankment. The news quickly spread throughout the surrounding villages. A large crowd witnessed the scene, as such a thing had happened for the first time in the area. Netra's wife and mother were inconsolable, and all the villagers were deeply affected. The police were informed, and the villagers testified that Netra was a kind, innocent man with no enemies. A foul play was the most unlikely reason, and the death must not be due to any cause like murder. Gailash was present throughout, keeping an eye over everything. He told the police as Netra suffered from epilepsy, he must have fallen into the water when no one was around. Netra's death must have been due to drowning. He went to great lengths in describing to the police the many virtues of Netra, like his simplicity, honesty, and good manners. He said he felt pity for the two female members of Netra's family and was worried about how they would be able to support themselves without Netra, who was the only male member of the household.

Everyone knew about Gailash's notoriety. Though married with children, he had kidnapped his wife's married sister from her in law's house. From his second wife, he had a few more children. He also tried living with his wife's elder sister but the woman did not stay with him for long. The villagers even claimed that Gailash had relationship with his mother-in-law too. But no one dared to stand against him as he worked for the police.

After a few months of Netra's death, people did not mention him as much in groups. The villagers believed that Netra's ghost was around. As children passed by the pond where the body was found, they would sprint a few meters on the embankment out of fear. At that time, the village had no electricity, and people used kerosene lanterns for lighting. Generally, the people went to bed early and woke up early at dawn. As the sun set, a thick veil of darkness would descend rapidly, and all activities in the village would stop. The village was full of dense forest-like vegetation, so it was natural for someone to be afraid to leave the house at night. After Netra's incident, the whole environment became frightful. Unless it was necessary, people preferred to stay confined to their houses after dusk. Otherwise, they would move in groups.

Gailash's first wife was talkative and proud of her husband's strength and capabilities. During a casual conversation with a village woman, she asked the woman if she would like to know the truth about Netra's death. She then explained how the problem started, and Gailash and his friends made a plan that ultimately led to fooling the police. It astonished the woman present there. After she left, the woman who heard from her spread the story of the murder of Netra all over the village like wildfire. All were taken by surprise. In respect of their love and affection for Netra, they sat for a meeting under the chairmanship of a village leader, Kiranjan Pradhan. Shri Pradhan was a clever man. He used to go to Balasore town and various government offices and know the legal processes. He took the initiative, mobilized the villagers and informed the Police about the murder case and the role of Gailash and his associates. The police, on reaching the village, asked for the remains of Netra's body, like bone and ashes. Before anything could happen, Gailash and his brother Gahana had reached the spot where the body had been cremated. They had prior information. They cleaned up the place, leaving no proof of his cremation.

The police took note of the names of the accused from the villagers. However, Gailash's wife denied having said anything to a village woman. The witness to the story was a woman named Mahya, who was the wife of Thakra. She was poor and used to beg alms from one house to another. She had constructed a small hut near Gailash's house on government land. Based on her testimony, Gailash and all the other accused were arrested and lodged in jail, facing a murder trial. After the police registered the case, the entire village came together and arranged funds through contributions to pay for the legal and other expenses. All the money was given to the leader, Kiranjan. Mahya was treated like a VIP and became a celebrity in the locality. She was carried in a palanquin on the shoulders of four men to the bus stop, from where she travelled by bus to Jaleswar town and by train to Balasore town. She was pampered and kept in good humour for the sake of justice in criminal case. As a result, she no longer needed to beg for survival.

However, Kiranjan began to deceive the villagers after a few court hearings. As usual, he accepted money from them for each hearing, but instead of attending court, he used the money to buy land in a village called Bagabali, which was 30 kilometres away from our village. He spent a lot of time there while the villagers thought he was attending to the court proceedings. When the complainants and witnesses did not show up in court, Gailash made a plea before the magistrate, claiming that the villagers were conspiring against him because they were jealous of his job as a police constable. He argued that they had falsely accused him and others in the case in an attempt to take away his job. As a result of the prosecution's repeated non-appearance in court, the magistrate released all the accused persons.

After release from the prison, Gailash arrived in the village carrying with him the fishing net on his shoulder, which had been seized and produced in the court as evidence of the murder of Netra. His brother Gahana and friend Kurendra were also with him. He was seen yelling and swearing all the way, taking the names of all the villagers who had grouped to send him to jail for killing Netra. He was giving open threats to all. Fearing him, the villagers hid from him for a few days. Gailash moved around the village with pride and arrogance like a lion.

As his first target, Gailash took on Thakra and his wife Mahya. He destroyed their hut and drove the couple away from the village. No one dared to stand in between and prevent him from doing so. The police department reinstated him as a constable, and he reported to the local police station for duty. From then, Gailash looked more powerful and became a kind of terror to the people of the locality. His influence was such that even after his death, his son got the job of constable who continued to dominate people.

Netra, one of the most innocent guys in the village, was killed due to suspicion of Kurendra. It was a fact that Faulati did not give Netra the silver coins. Even in her imagination, she never thought of doing so, though she took his name to cause irritation to his brother-in-law Kurendra. Faulati had her plans, which she never revealed. It was believed that she gave all her husband's share of properties and wealth to her brothers and came to live in her brothers' house. She gave nothing to Netra and his family. Following the death of Netra, his wife and mother lived miserably for several years. The descendants of Judra Das provided little support from time to time, barely for survival.

The story of Netra was a case study for everyone in the village. People were naturally terrified as no one was punished after a murder. The murderers were seen living with pride and dignity. After the incident, no one in the area would be allowed to go outside home alone, and movement after dusk was very limited. They would return from the market just before the evening. If there was any personal enmity with someone, the powerful side would threaten the other side with dire consequences. They would threaten to repeat another incident like Gailash did to Netra.

The police outpost was located quite far from the village, which had poor road communication and no vehicles to reach. Only a few people had bicycles, and most people travelled on foot. In this situation, Gailash was the only person who could help get police support. However, people were afraid to be witnesses, fearing reprisal. They felt that influential people could commit heinous crimes like murder and still get away with it without facing any punishment. The old structures of power and traditional dominance dominated the village environment. People hardly dared to protest against the rich and powerful, even if their behaviour was unjustified. If a poor person dared stand up against the rich, he would be ostracized. No one would engage them as a labourer, and they would be boycotted from ritual and ceremonial occasions, too. In the event of an excommunication, the survival of a family would become extremely painful and depend on the mercy of God. As a result, everyone had to surrender before the powerful elements of the village to survive.

The story of Netra had a profound impact on our family. We always lived in fear due to the hostility of our neighbours, who had the backing of a powerful group. As children, we anxiously awaited our father's return from work, praying for his safety. Our enemies made several attempts to attack him on his way back home late at night. Whenever we had to go outside, we would travel as a family, protecting each other. My mother never allowed me to go to the village pond where men and women, including young people, would bathe. She was scared that someone might harm me by drowning me. As a result, I could not learn how to swim, while all my friends became adept at it in childhood. I learnt it much later. Our survival was a matter of sheer luck.

Netra's story provides insight into the situation in our village when my parents were at loggerheads with our neighbours. The latter intended to evict us from the village and had the backing of the most influential group of people, as explained later in the narration. Although some villagers sympathized with us, they chose to remain neutral and not confront our enemies.

N.B.: The story is based on facts. However, due to their sensitive nature, the characters have been masked.

3

A Dark Tunnel and Light at the End

At the time of India's independence, some of our national leaders had a romantic view of the village system in the country. They believed that villages were self-reliant and independent units. Villagers had been resolving their issues amicably through their meetings since time immemorial. The elder members of the community were a highly respected group who were entrusted with the responsibility of delivering justice. The system was not expensive and was closely connected to the people. The villages were autonomous and should continue to remain so, with minimal interference from external sources after independence. However, a closer look reveals a different reality. The decision-making process was far from democratic. The powerful members of the community often influenced the decisions, and smaller groups, formed based on caste, kinship, and lineage, usually worked in their self-interests. The decision-makers were typically from the upper echelons of the society, and they had the blessings of the priestly class. They were not immune to favouritism and the concepts of liberty, equality, and fraternity were foreign to them. They knew how to manipulate one group against the other with ease. The dispute-resolution process in village meetings was not democratic, and the seating arrangements followed a caste hierarchy. Women had no voice and there was no reference to any written law and precedence. The aggrieved party had to accept the decision, with no appeal or review process available. If a sanction was imposed against a family, its survival would be impossible and anyone opposing the decision would face dire consequences, including death. Despite the introduction of the new panchayati raj system by the government, the old panchayati raj system remained functional. The story of my family serves as a case study of how the village system in older times was unfair and could not be accepted as an authority to deliver justice in modern times, even though it had served several purposes for centuries.

My village and the surrounding region have a long history of being part of the ancient Kalinga kingdom in eastern India. In 1803, the Balasore district became a British territory. Some people feel proud that the Marathas gained control of our area from the Muslims before the British conquest. However, the administration during the Maratha rule was not favourable to the people. There was mismanagement everywhere, and lower-level officials under the Maratha rulers committed atrocities and subjected our people to several exploitations. As a result, the rule under a Hindu empire became intolerable to the inhabitants due to the ruthlessness. The British slowly moved to establish their supremacy on Odisha's soil by connecting the territory over the east coast, which facilitated their trade and commerce. By then, the fragile and weak Maratha administration provided a fertile ground for the British to realize their ambition of establishing their authority over Odisha. On 4 October 1803, the route from Balasore to Cuttack was cleared by the British soldiers. Colonel Ferguson had marched from Jaleswar to Balasore, and they undertook an operation to the north-east of the Subarnarekha river. One Captain Lamb occupied Pataspur, Kamarda, Bhograi (my area), Shahbandar, and Jamukunda on Colonel Fenwick's orders. Through a combination of conciliatory and coercive measures, the zamindars were brought under British control. On 17 December 1803, Raghuji Bhonsle ceded Balasore to the East India Company through the Deogaon Treaty. Finally, the British occupied Odisha in 1803, and Balasore came under the Bengal Presidency. The people of the older generation used to appreciate the British rule over the Maratha rule. At the time of independence, our people welcomed the new era with great joy and hope for a new beginning. However, the old system continued for some decades and there was great delay for the real change to take place at the ground level.

My village Narasinghapur is in the Bhograi block of the Balasore district. It is situated on the border of Odisha and neighbouring Bengal state. For a long time, our village had better connectivity with Bengal than with Odisha. It was only after 1936, with the formation of a separate state of Odisha, that our village got a well-demarcated border. Most probably, our village was a new settlement area for the people who had migrated from Bengal at some point in time during the last three hundred years. Being so close to the coastline, our area is often subjected to natural calamities like cyclones. Each cyclone brought untold misery to the people. Due to the construction of a coast canal and an adjoining high embankment, a new physical barrier was created during the British rule between the two parts of the coastal area towards the end of the nineteenth century. While our area was very close to the coastline, full of sand dunes, the other side got protection from cyclones but remained water-logged due to the slower discharge of rainwater and river drainage to the sea during the rainy season. The situation has changed significantly after a period of more than one hundred years. To connect both parts of our block area, it took about a hundred years to construct a bridge over the coast canal. The construction of the bridge was not permitted by the order of the British government earlier so as not to obstruct the canal navigation. I saw the bridge construction during my childhood.

The road to Digha town in Bengal was laid from the coast canal in Batagram village, allowing for communication and vehicular transportation. Prior to this, there was no modern means of transport. The great famine of 1866 had devastated a large part of Bengal and Odisha, resulting in the death of over one-third of the population due to hunger and starvation. After this, a coast canal was built, bringing attention to irrigation, trade, commerce, and movement. Subsequently, the British government established railway communication on the East Coast. However, by 1928, the investment in the coast canal was deemed infeasible and wasteful due to its low profitability and associated problems and thus was abandoned. As a result, the condition of the coast canal deteriorated over time and it is languishing today. There are often demands for its restoration for navigation purposes. During British rule, our area was exposed to modern civilization, education, and modern ideas. However, buses did not begin operating in our area until the early 1970s, long after independence. Before that, only limited bus services were available from Batagram village to Jaleswar town, allowing our people to travel to urban areas. Until the early 1980s, most villagers had never seen a train despite Jaleswar being only about 30 kilometres away. Our people had no business or relationships beyond a few neighbouring villages, making it truly a backward area. As a child, my initial few years were like living on an island.

My village was sparsely populated until the 1980s. The houses were mostly semi-permanent; they had thick mud walls, mud floors, and thatched roofs. Some of the mud houses were even double-storied, with the first floor built over strong wooden beams on very wide mud walls. A few houses like ours had tiled roofing. Skilled artisans used to build such strong houses in the rural areas, capable of withstanding several cyclones, heavy downpours, and waterlogging. However, the conditions of the poorer households were pathetic. The houses were separated from each other by ponds, paddy fields, and horticultural gardens. Only two to three rich households had buildings made of brick walls and concrete roofing. The traditional system of caste dominance was in full force.

Earlier, domestic animals like goats, sheep, and chickens were considered impure by the villagers. Only cows and bullocks were permitted. The economy was purely agriculture based. As the land for paddy cultivation was limited, the villagers cleared the forested area and levelled the sand dunes to put up betel leaf vines, which were the largest source of income and employment. There was no source of irrigation. People used to dig shallow tube wells of a few feet to get drinking water.

My father Bhajahari was born in 1932, which was four years before the separate state of Odisha was formed. A primary school has been functioning in my village since 1892. This was the only place of education for the local children in the undivided Odisha and Bengal states. Even till the 1970s, the school used to get children from the Bengal side, and they had no difficulty getting a job either in Odisha or Bengal. However, such practice has been stopped after the West Bengal government emphasized on Bengali language and opened schools on its side. Even though the people in the neighbouring villages in West Bengal are Odia-speaking, they have stopped learning Odia. The common people started feeling the existence of a political boundary much later between the bordering villages. Long before my father's time, his grandfather had migrated from a village named Kainada, in Bengal, and was settled here. My father was a brilliant student. Those days, if anyone was bright, he would be picked up for teaching in elementary classes by the government after minor school education. The literacy rate was very poor then and it was hard to find educated people opting to become a primary school teacher. Unfortunately, my father had to drop out after primary standard as his father died at a young age of about thirty. His mother suffered from asthma and would be bedridden most of the time. His elder brother became mentally ill at a very young age. Except for wage labour, the family had no other source of livelihood. By the time my father turned ten, he had to shoulder the responsibility of looking after a family of three. He worked as a labourer and travelled long distances on barefoot to purchase paddy from a market in Jaleswar town, 30 kilometres away. He would get the paddy boiled and dried under the sun. Afterwards, taking the help of some village women, he would get the paddy milled using a traditional device called *dhenki*. The device is usually made of a single piece of hardwood of about seven feet. The slender wooden body is fixed on a fulcrum dividing the body into two unequal parts. When using dhenki, one person would apply pressure to one end, causing the longer end to lift and allowing a free fall. This motion, along with the force of the device's weight, separates the rice from the brown husk. Normally, two people operate the mill. The rice would be sold locally, and some profit would be generated. This was the time much before the green revolution reached our area. Fresh in his memory was the death of several people in the area due to starvation following a very severe cyclone, flooding, and loss of paddy crops.

Food grains were very scarce, and cultivating a single crop of paddy was dependent on rainfall, as there was no source of irrigation in the area. Productivity was very low compared to present times. Poor rainfall, droughts, cyclones, and floods created famine-like situations at regular intervals. The season of scarcity would begin after the transplantation of paddy until its ripening and harvest. During this four-month period, the poor faced the greatest stress. Unfortunately, this was also the time for cyclones, floods, and droughts, which caused further problems. The rich harvested more paddy and had enough stock to sustain themselves throughout the year. They used the surplus paddy to lend money with exorbitant interest rates to others. Most of the people who took loans were unable to repay, which led to the rich appropriating land, ornaments, and utensils. The poor became even poorer, and some of them ended up as bonded labour. At that time, the village had hardly thirty households and there were no good opportunities for even seasonal labour work. Some villagers cleared forested sandy areas and set up betel leaf vines.

My father, facing difficulty in earning enough money to support his family, joined other youths of his village, 24 Parganas, West Bengal, on the outskirts of Kolkata, to work as a domestic agricultural labourer. At that time, this was a rural area with vast agricultural land and an insufficient number of working-class people. The landlord was pleased with my father's manners, sincerity, and hard work. He treated him like a son and was very kind to him. He even offered him land and other support to settle there. However, my father had to politely refuse the offer and return to the village after a few years because his mother and brother needed his support back at home.

The country eventually gained independence. My father got married by paying a bride price to my mother's father with the money he had earned in Bengal. The dowry system was not widely prevalent in the area at that time. Due to societal bias against daughters, there were fewer girls than boys, which meant many men remained unmarried. In those days, people got married at a very young age. For instance, my mother was barely nine years old when she got married and as per the customs, she stayed in her father's place till the time she reached puberty. My father, on the other hand, lived in his village and took care of his mother and elder brother. He had to leave the village to earn money and provide for his mother and brother's basic needs.

My mother, too, was not very fortunate at birth. Her father preferred sons over daughters and was upset when a second girl child was born in the family. He was so angry and frustrated at her birth that he contemplated leaving her in the forest. The cruel man had no qualms about the newborn being eaten away by wild animals. However, her not-so-unkind uncle came to the rescue and dissuaded my grandfather against it, and eventually, better sense prevailed upon him. My grandfather was of the opinion that girls were liabilities to a family, and so they should be married off in a few years. The Hindu Succession Act came into force only in the year 1956, and before that, girls had no legal rights and had no share in the ancestral property. After one year of her birth, my uncle was born, giving much relief to my grandfather. While my uncle was pampered and sent to school, it remained a distant dream for my mother. Till the time my mother lived in her parental house, she worked in the family paddy field and contributed to household chores. She would also bring food and water for the labourers working in the family field. As per the prevailing societal norms of that time, very few girls were sent to schools, and my grandfather, too, believed that girls did not need to be educated. When my father's family sent a marriage proposal to her father, he did not agree initially. My father's family was poor, without any means of income or agricultural land. However, when a bride price of ₹60 was offered, he agreed to the proposal out of greed. No one asked my mother if she was willing for the marriage. My mother had two sisters and my grandfather did not take any bride price when they were married off as their husbands were rich. My grandfather did not love my mother and treated her differently. He believed that he would get salvation only when his son performed all the rituals on his death. However, my uncle dropped out of school early in his life. He tried his hand in agriculture and small business but was not successful. When he was old, his condition became worse and he died a poor man.

When my mother came of age to live with my father, her mother-in-law had already passed away. Her unruly brother-in-law would torture her. He had been married but when he got afflicted with mental illness, his wife deserted him. My father tried to persuade her to come back but failed. She remarried, leaving her little son behind. My mother's elder sister, who lived in West Bengal, had no child of her own.

She adopted the child. Over a short period of time, my uncle's mental illness became worse. People feared to go near him but my father was extremely patient with him. Once, my uncle beat my father so severely that it was only my father's good luck that he survived. My uncle never received any medical treatment for his illness as it was feared that such sick people were confined to cells of mental hospitals in faraway places. After a few years, my uncle passed away.

The old mud house in my village was quite uninhabitable. My father's elder brother would damage the floor, wall, and roof of the house at regular intervals, causing further problems. My father would repair it soon after. Faced with many challenges, my parents made efforts to bring positive changes in their lives through hard labour. My father had a maternal grandmother who had no son to be her legal heir. She gifted and registered all her properties in my father's name. Instead of moving to his grandmother's village, my parents decided to sell off the inherited property. With the money thus earned, my father bought some land in his own village. Within a very short period of time, my parents became well off and recognized. They set up betel leaf vines and cultivated paddy crops on the newly acquired land. As the income rose, my father stopped going out with his neighbours to work as a wage labourer in agriculture fields and betel leaf vines. Rather, he needed people to work for him. In those days, since no one would work in the house of a scheduled caste person, labourers from lower-caste and Muslim communities from far away areas in West Bengal would come to help them in agriculture activities on a wage labour basis. My parents reared two lovely bullocks, fondly naming them Kalia and Chanda, for cultivation operation. The house was upgraded with Mangalorean tile roofing, giving them a newfound status. Soon there was happiness and smiles in the family.

After my parent's social and economic status improved, they started mingling with influential people in the village. My father was asked to volunteer and serve milk to school children. The government was supplying milk under foreign aid to meet the nutritional needs of the school children. During that time, the villagers were highly involved in the school operation. The teachers were subservient to the villagers, who interfered in every school-related decision. The villagers repaired and maintained the school building and even donated teachers' chairs. The donors' names would be boldly painted on the chairs to glorify them. The school committee would organize feasts during occasions like Ganesh Puja and Saraswati Puja and farewell ceremonies for retiring teachers. The government seemed to be withdrawn from day-to-day functioning. Later, my father was disengaged from the milk distribution duty when the upper caste complained about his unclean caste and his being untouchable.

Every evening, my father read holy scriptures like the Mahabharata and Puranas in Odia and Bengali. My elder sister and mother would listen to him carefully. My mother had no formal education. My father motivated her to learn to read and write, and soon she was able to read and write in Odia and Bengali. She, too, started reading from the holy scriptures daily. She was very religious and believed in good karma. She was very judicious in her words, thoughts, and actions.

Since 1954, a man named Ananta Das had been a ward member of our village, Narasinghapur. He was the most powerful decision-maker in the area and well-known in the locality. He belonged to an influential community who were well known and engaged in the cultivation of betel leaf. This community had good expertise in growing this cash crop, for which the area was well recognized. That was a time when government officers rarely visited rural areas or interfered in village matters. Whether it was under the Maratha rule or the British, the village had hardly seen any outside interference as long as land revenue was paid to the zamindar through intermediaries in the past. The zamindars had their own army and would use force for the collection of land revenue. Because of the unique roles they played, they remained deeply rooted in the system despite the transfer of power from one group to another. The traditional village leadership tradition also remained intact. The land tax was too much before the independence. Some poor people were reluctant to have government land recorded in their names by the settlement officers for fear of not being able to pay the taxes and face the ruthless tax collectors appointed by the zamindars. The poor people had the fear of incurring huge costs and putting great labour to make the land arable by clearing trees and bushes and levelling it before cultivating. The rich people worked with the settlement officers to get the government land settled in their names as the production system worked in their favour. The caste-based traditional and feudal structure in the village was in full control.

In 1957, Durga Shankar Das from neighbouring Taladi Mouza became the MLA from the Bhograi constituency. He belonged to the Congress party, the most favoured party in the area because of its role in India's independence. On the ground level, Ananta Das, Trilochan Das, and Laxmikant Jena wielded their power and influence. Their decisions were the last word in the village and were enforced ruthlessly. Anyone who dared to oppose their decision would face dire consequences. Niranjan Pradhan, another shrewd man from the adjoining village, would often join this powerful group at his convenience. He was adept at using people for his benefit. These four men planned activities that best suited their interests.

The next state assembly election was held in 1961. That year, the Congress party lost the election, and Pyarimohan Das from the Praja Socialist Party of Taladi Mouza became the new MLA. The village was divided over party politics, with villagers speaking ill of the previous ward members and other leaders. Ananta Das asked my father to enter the gram panchayat election and become a ward member. However, my father politely refused the offer as he did not want to hurt his friend Laxmikanta Jena, who was more politically active and willing. This annoyed Ananta Das, who did not like my father's defiance. Trilochan Das then proposed the name of Laxmikanta Jena from the Praja Socialist Party as the candidate. He easily got the support of my father's hostile neighbours and got elected. After the election, the disputes in the village continued. People remained divided into several small groups, and the personal issues of individuals would often flare up unnecessarily.

My parents were frequently targeted by our jealous neighbours who did not like my father's newly acquired status. They were upset with him being offered a nomination for ward member from the Congress party and his association with influential people of the village. Due to our changed circumstances, my father no longer accompanied them for labour work, which further infuriated them. They would often quarrel with my mother on flimsy pretexts and even threatened to attack my father. My grandfather had three brothers. On the east side of our house lived Laxmikanta, who was the only son of one of my grandfather's brothers. On the west side, four sons from another brother lived. The houses were adjoined to each other, separated by a physical barricade. Laxmikanta's wife would often bicker with my mother and taunt her for not having given birth to a son. The cantankerous lady would often hurt my mother by reminding her of her three newborns, who had died a few months after their birth. During those days, villages did not have access to modern medical facilities, institutional delivery, and prenatal and post-natal care systems. As a result, infant mortality rates were very high. To combat this, traditional healers called kabiraj were in high demand. It was believed that if a family did not have a son, they were considered cursed. Society would go to a great extent to break a woman psychologically and make her feel guilty for not having given birth to a male child.

In our village, superstitions and strange beliefs were rampant. The villagers believed in a demigod named Yaksha. They thought he could appear anywhere, including village roads or ponds, carrying a huge pole at night. It was believed that he was the guardian of wealth, including the wealth of our ancestors that was kept in several huge brass pots. It was thought that he walked behind the pots that rolled forward in a row, and the silver and gold coins in those pots would make a unique metallic sound. Many villagers claimed to have encountered Yaksha. When my parents started living a comfortable life, the neighbours said it was because they received wealth from Yaksha through an act of deception. As a result, their children were dying because of Yaksha's curse.

My mother became depressed and wanted to drown herself in the waters of the Bay of Bengal, a few kilometres away from our home, and end all her sufferings. One day, a local villager informed my father about my mother's one such attempt. He immediately rushed to the seashore and rescued her. My mother had become disturbed and too pessimistic about life. Unfortunately, no treatment was available in the village. The immediate neighbours, too, would unite, scold, and abuse my parents in unparliamentary words. Village meetings would be called on small pretexts to humiliate my parents and force them to apologize for no wrongs committed. My father would yield to their demands to appease them. Ananta Das would incite our neighbours to commit more crime. My father had a one-third claim on a joint property that belonged to his grandfather. This included rights over a common fish pond, several coconuts, and other fruit-bearing trees. The neighbours would catch fish from the pond and refuse to give him his share. It was rather fun for them to see that my parents suffered and got humiliated.

Killing a person was easy in those gory days. The criminals could go unpunished. If powerful people were involved, there would be no witnesses. Often, Netra's unsolved murder case would be cited as an example to drive home fear into the minds of gullible and marginalized people. Drawing lessons from the murder case of Netra, our neighbours hatched a plan to kill my father. They planned to drown him in the common fish pond and invited him to join them in catching fish. However, a well-wisher warned my father about the group's devious plan. My father thus escaped an attempt on his life.

My family owned a fish pond. One day at midnight, a neighbour poisoned its water. The next morning all the fish in the pond were found dead. Looking at the dead fish, many feeble-hearted onlookers burst into tears. The village leaders were summoned to render assistance. However, they rejected the claim that a villager could have poisoned the pond water and instead opined that a meteor must have fallen into the water causing the fish to die. The village leaders always supported our neighbours. If they had taken heed of my parents' complaint, then the police would have been involved, which would lead to further probing and action.

The agricultural practice was to harvest manually and leave the paddy stock along with straw in the open paddy field for a few days to dry. Often, in the dark hours of the night, the neighbours would destroy the harvested paddy in the field. To irritate and provoke the family, they would catch fish from the common pond regularly and not give my father his share. My mother complained to the local sarpanch. The sarpanch came to the village to resolve the issue. However, our neighbours bribed the Gram Rakshi, and as a result, he lied to the sarpanch that no one from our family was present at home. Without settling the matter, the sarpanch left.

After the evening hours, villagers rarely visited each other's homes. Without electricity, the village would be pitch dark. At that time, no one could hear any cries or screams. Taking advantage of the situation, two of our neighbours Bhanu and Bada Baya would torment us routinely. They were well-built, muscular, and in the prime of their youth. They would routinely harass us in the middle of the night, causing terror and distress. To protect themselves and their three little children, my parents would flee the house, leaving it unlocked, seeking refuge from friendly neighbours who belonged to the upper caste.

Bhanu was skilled in pelting bullets made of clay. Villagers used them to scare monkeys away. The bullets were made by mixing clay and water and then dried in the sun. The clay balls would harden like bullets. Bhanu used these bullets against us. We got hit by these bullets many times. The pain would be unbearable, and healing took time. Our bodies still bear the marks. It has become a routine affair. Our adversaries took feedback from the assailants and planned their next move. They would often say, 'Let us break the ego of a Harijan man who is trying to become famous and powerful'. Such events were not restricted to night only. In the daytime too, we could be seen fleeing our house owing to sudden, unprovoked attacks. We could return to our home only after getting assistance from the gram rakshi and Laxmikanta Jena, the ward member. Not only our pond but also our food had been poisoned.

My father, unable to take such torments anymore, disappeared one day. He did not inform anyone, including my mother. It was a nightmare for my mother. In addition to taking care of three little children, she had to search for my father. Unable to find any clue, she broke down. She would weep while listening to the taunts and bitter words of the neighbourhood women. She was under so much agony that their bitter words were of no effect. One of the elderly women in the neighbourhood would throw objects on her cowshed roof and then yell that my father's ghost had returned to the village to haunt her and other women. Her objective was to say that my father had died. She would hurl her choicest abuses at my parents for hours. Other women would also join her. They would stop only when their throats went sore. However, after a few days, my father returned. He had gone to Puri. My mother's joy knew no bounds when she saw him.

This did not stop the neighbours, though. They continued their verbal and physical attacks. To scare our neighbours, my father hatched a plan. He started calling himself 'Puri Babaji' and behaved as if he had gone mad. He knew even if he accidentally hurt anyone, there would be no punishment for a madman.

To avoid encountering the tormentors, the little pathway on the front of our house was closed permanently. The family took the backside leading through the muddy paddy field to travel. Before leaving for West Bengal to work as a labourer, my father had handed a piece of land to a neighbour. One day, when he asked the man politely to return the land, he was hurled abuses. The man had almost hit my father with a huge bamboo stick in a fit of rage. It was only because the gram rakshi was present that my father could escape. Years later, during the land settlement operation, the neighbour, with the help of some villagers, got the land recorded clandestinely in his name.

The situation was becoming unbearable and worse for us. People were not allowed to work in our betel vine and land. We were in constant fear of being physically assaulted and killed. My parents worried for their small children's lives. As a consequence, the land remained fallow and the betel vine had to be pulled down. My parents had, in the meantime, become Shri Chaitanya Maha Prabhu's devotees. They were indoctrinated by a local guru named Radhakrishna Pal. Looking at our poor plight, the guru and his son Adaitya came to the house. They convinced my parents to leave the village and resettle somewhere else. Radhakrishna Pal cited Lord Krishna's example, who was also forced to leave Mathura and settle in Dwarka. They advised my parents to sell all their land in the village to them. My father had total faith in his guru. Moreover, they were not left with any other alternatives. My parents decided to settle in West Bengal, where my mother's sister lived. Radhakrishna Pal agreed to pay ₹13,000, a huge sum in 1969, for the entire land. He also promised to pay an additional sum of ₹150 for our two bullocks. This sum would have been sufficient to buy seven acres of land in West Bengal. With this thought, my father visited Shipur Mouza of West Bengal and made an informal agreement with the landowner to purchase the land.

My father went to the sub-registrar's office in the nearby Jaleswar town with two witnesses, Shridhar Dhamudia and Surendra Giri of the locality. Adaita Pal got the land registered in his name and paid a part sum of ₹3,900. He promised to pay the remaining amount at the time when my father was ready to buy the land in West Bengal. The argument was that it would not be safe for my father to keep so much money, and he might squander it away. My father trusted the guru and his son completely. The witnesses who had signed the sale deeds were aware of the details. In the court, it was declared that my father had been paid the full amount upon which the registration deed was executed. Three days later, Adaita got the sales documents from the sub-registrar's office. My father went to Shipur Mouza of Medinipur district to fix the modalities and date for purchasing land there. In the meanwhile, Radhakrishna Pal had a change of mind. He lied to the villagers that he had paid my father the entire amount and had no more liabilities against my father. Upon hearing this, my father summoned the witnesses. The two gentlemen confronted Radhakrishna Pal, but it was of no avail. Rather, Radhakrishna Pal became aggressive. He and his extended family members outnumbered us. He forcefully started cultivating our land. He would enter our homestead and pluck coconut, jackfruit, and other fruits and vegetables from there. He took away the bullocks. My father was forced to stay inside the house. A friendly neighbour, Bijay Dhamudia, helped the family buy grain and other essential items for several months. Late at night, when the entire village was in deep sleep, my father would walk to the weekly market, 5 kilometres away, to buy things. He would be the last customer in the haat. He would avoid regular routes and instead took longer and secluded paths to avoid attacks.

Finding no other way and help, my father decided to shift the entire family to the faraway town of Puri. He hoped to survive by begging for alms in front of the Jagannath temple. The family stayed in Puri for a few days. In the meantime, the local administration was intimated about the family's disappearance. The family was located in Puri and brought back to the village. Back in the village, Pal and his supporters encouraged our neighbours to harass and chase us away with the promise that our homestead land would be given to them free. Bhanu took the lead and within a few hours of us reaching home, he started pelting clay bullets that injured us. I still bear the marks of the injury on my body. Apart from clay bullets, brickbats and chunks of dried clay were also hurled at us. Fearing for our life, we again ran away from the village. We could return only with the support of sympathetic men and women. While we were away, our enemies had poisoned our food. We remained hungry till a kind-hearted villager gave food to us. Sympathetic villagers and Laxmikant Jena, the ward member, complained to the police. A meeting was held in the presence of police and villagers, where Radhakrishna Pal admitted to having made a partial payment. The police instructed him to pay my father the promised amount so that he could buy the proposed land in Shipur Mouza of Medinipur without further delay. The police also opened the road on the front side of our house. We were able to move out easily once again. The police instructed the gram rakshi to protect and help us.

Our neighbours bore more grudge against my mother than my father. My father was a tolerant, peace-loving man who prayed that God would help him out. He would remain quiet even at the worst kind of provocation. He believed that as the neighbours were from his extended family, they would one day realize their wrongdoings. In contrast, my mother would confront our enemies to protect the family. She would reply to the provocations and keep the enemies under check. Though the path was opened in the front by the police, life remained difficult for us. Whenever my parents passed through it, the neighbours would try to provoke them by taunting and hurling abusive language at them. They gathered in small groups and were even prepared to attack us in case we reacted.

One afternoon, a girl from the neighbourhood threw garbage inside our courtyard. Following this, a heated quarrel broke out between our family and hers. After the quarrel had subsided a few hours later, my mother went out. My elder sister, barely six years old, was her usual companion. An hour or so later, when my mother and sister were returning, Bhanu's wife spotted them. When my mother was at arm's length, she grabbed her hair and pushed her down with full force. Like Bhanu, his wife was also a strong lady. A few more ladies joined her in the attack. My sister started calling my father. Hearing her voice, my father rushed out of the house and pleaded to the women for their mercy. But he was overpowered. Unable to protect my mother, he left her at their mercy, hoping better sense would prevail over them. The attackers continued to assault my mother and left only when she dropped unconscious and was almost dead. My sister was witness to the harrowing event and was traumatized. Being a year old, I was too small to remember the details. After the attackers left her motionless, my father picked her up. She lay motionless for four days on our veranda without any medicine or aid.

On the fifth day, my father was able to arrange a palanquin with incredible difficulty. Four people carried my mother to her sister's place in Medinipur. On the way, she received treatment at Chandanpur Hospital in West Bengal. When my mother was being carried away, Radhakrishna Pal and his family hurled abuses at us while continuing to till our land. The doctors at Chandanpur Hospital repeatedly asked about the names of persons who attacked my mother so that they could inform the police in West Bengal. But my father did not reveal their names. He even prevailed upon the little children not to reveal anything. To date, we cannot understand the motive behind our father's actions. My mother was taken to her sister's house in Shipur, West Bengal. Her sister took good care of her. It took more than a few months for my mother to recover completely. After my mother had fully recovered, we returned to our village. During our absence, Bhanu lodged a case against my father at the police outpost. The complaint said that my father had gone mad and attacked eight women, including his wife.

A few days later, another village meeting was called upon our return. My father invited my mother's relatives for support. The witnesses to the registration were asked to give their version. Pal was urged to return all the land and properties to my father as he had not paid the consideration money. Adaita Pal and Radhakrishna Pal consented to it, but Gobind Pal, another crooked person in the family, prevailed upon them, and as a result, the meeting became unsuccessful.

The atmosphere continued to remain tense. One day, early in the morning, we saw Radhakrishna Pal and his workers tilling their land while our land remained fallow due to the dispute. One could only imagine the anguish my parents must have gone through for not being able to cultivate their land and feed their little children. Frustrated, my parents went to meet Pal to ask for our dues. For self-protection, my father carried an axe called kuradhi and my mother dabali, a tool fitted to cut coconut. An altercation followed. Pal and his workers surrounded my parents and beat them very badly. They were thrown into the muddy water. In a fit of rage and to protect herself, my mother hit Gadadhar Pal with the dabali. In the next moment, my parents were tied with ropes and dragged to Pal's house. All the villagers gathered to witness the ghastly scene. Our neighbours, too, joined Pal's group. They urged Pal to kill my parents. It was the saddest day of our life. We were filled with sorrow, pain, fear, anguish, and tears. However, some upright villagers confronted Pal and asked him to return our dues. But Pal remained unmoved as he was filled with greed. He even lodged a case against us, alleging that my parents had attacked him and his workers. A criminal case was filed.

My parents received summons from the Balasore court. Balasore is 80 kilometres away from our village. One had to walk 8 kilometres on foot to catch a bus at Batagram. After travelling more than 20 km, one would reach Jaleswar, from where one boarded the train. Again, a few kilometres needed to be walked from the Balasore station to reach Kutchery. My parents had no place to sleep or rest and were ordered to attend court every seven days. With great difficulty, we would attend every court date. My mother used to carry my younger sister, still a toddler, in her arms. My father would carry me on his shoulder. My elder sister would walk and also carry a few things. Food and dress were bundled together and carried by my father on his back. We hardly had any possessions, barring a few bare necessities. After returning home, my mother would pump water from the hand pump. She would drink it first and wait to see if it had any adverse effect on her. If she felt fine, then we would drink. It was my mother's conscious decision to become the guinea pig each time to ensure her family remained safe. She was always ready to die for all of us.

As luck would have it, the case would get adjourned. After a few appearances, my father stopped attending the court. As a result, the court issued an arrest warrant against my father. The police came at noon to arrest my father. He was not allowed to eat his meal. Feeling utterly helpless, my mother followed the police with the three of us. She was crying all the way. The outpost was 5 kilometres away. We waited outside the outpost. From the outpost, my father was taken to the Jaleswarpur police station. Hearing this news, one of the influential villagers from my mother's parental village came to the police station to release my father on bail. However, my father's bail was refused. Instead, my father was handcuffed and made to board a bus. My mother, too, along with us, boarded the same bus. She had become almost mad. Seeing our plight, a few people offered us food and money. The bus conductor did not dare to ask for fare from my mother. Then, like my father and policeman, we also took the train from Jaleswar to Balasore. My father was lodged in Balasore jail, and we spent the night in the open field. Some lawyers and clerks came to know about our plight and donated some money like we were beggars. The next day, my father was produced before the presiding officer, who was then called the sub-divisional magistrate. The presiding officer reprimanded the police for handcuffing my father as he was not a criminal but rather a victim. A friend from the neighbouring village was present in court that day. He agreed to stand as surety, and my father was released.

We had to make regular court visits from 1970 to 1972. Money is needed for any judicial proceedings. Apart from paying the lawyer and clerk, money was also needed for travelling. To avoid spending any money on food, we carried puffed rice, the cheapest food available to the poor people in the area. To make the puffed rice soft, it was held in a gamcha and water was sprinkled on it. My parents were forced to travel to the court with their three children. It would have been dangerous to leave any family member alone in the village or for my father to travel alone. To meet the expenses, my father started selling the household items one by one. The last thing he sold was my brass plate. On that day, my mother cried inconsolably. We were left with nothing. We had become paupers.

On each day of the hearing, we only met the private clerk called 'moharir'. The government advocate would come very late, just before the court proceeding. The moharir would brief us about the happenings in the court at the end of the day. He would inform us of the next hearing date or suggest the next course of action. After several hearings, the court cancelled the sale deed executed between my father and Pal on the grounds that the consideration amount had not been paid. Adaita Pal was very unhappy with the decision. As he had paid a part of the agreed amount, he wanted my father to sell him again two plots of our land. Ominously, Adaita Pal felt ill and died the next day. My parents did not want to sell any land to Pal's family and even wanted to return the part money. However, Gadadhar Pal, Adaita's son, played tricks and was successful in deceiving my father again. He tricked my father into going to Balasore under the pretext that the matter needed further settlement. With the help of advocates, Gadadhar Pal forcibly got two of our plots registered in his name.

My parents were deceived again. Acting on advice, my father filed a case against Gadadhar Pal. He wanted his land back. These two land plots, locally called Baunsabadi and Dholpura, became symbolic of our legal fight. As a mark of protest, my father did not cultivate the remaining land, which we got back following the cancellation of the previous sale deed by the court. He believed that his case would become weak if he cultivated them. As a result, the land remained fallow for twenty-seven years while the case relating to the restoration of two plots from the possession of Pal was being heard in Balasore.

Twenty-seven years of deprivation is a long period of time. My siblings and I were growing up and needed food and care. We did not have adequate clothing and would shiver during winter. My sisters were forced to drop out of school to handle household chores while my parents went out to earn a livelihood. My elder sister sacrificed her education so that I could continue mine. My father had to travel to Balasore regularly to attend to the court case. The neighbours became less virulent and received no support from Pal and others. As we were already living in dismal poverty, they felt their objective had been achieved. They tried to have a normal relationship with us after more than two decades, and we consented.

In 1999, under Section 59 (1) of the Odisha Land Reforms Act, the case came for hearing before Ashwini Kumar Vaishnaw, the then collector of Balasore, against the order of an additional district magistrate. As my father belonged to the scheduled castes, any transfer of his land would be valid only when the sub-collector gave permission. This procedure was not followed during the second land transfer. The additional district magistrate observed that Adaita Pal had taken permission to buy land from my father on 31 December 1970. After his sudden death, his son Gadadhar Pal used the same permission letter to buy the two plots of land in 1972. The court said that the permission granted in favour of selling land to a person is non-transferrable and lapses after their death. To come to this decision, it took the courts almost three decades.

It was a momentous moment in my parents' lives to get legal possession of their land. In their fight for what was their due, they had been pushed into the abyss of poverty. They had struggled to make ends meet or provide food, clothes, and education to their children. In this difficult journey, they remained steadfast in their belief in the supreme power and never lost hope of getting justice.

My parents' struggles and sufferings had a profound impact on me. I wanted to grow a strong man and take revenge on all those who had wreaked havoc on my family. My family followed a pescatarian diet, but I insisted that I be allowed to eat meat. My mother gave in to my demand, but my father was unhappy with the decision. But now, looking back, my outlook has changed. I feel I did not need to seek any revenge. Those who wronged us also suffered. Advaita Pal died a sudden death. Gobind Pal suffered from illness and died a painful death. The others languished in poverty and survived on government doles. Instead, I became instrumental in getting much-needed assistance for their sustenance.

Bhanu's family abandoned him in old age. He committed suicide. His wife, too, was abandoned by her children. She suffered from asthma and died in pathetic condition. The dispute in Bada Baya's family continued over generations. Bada Baya pushed his father to his death. He faced ill treatment from his children in old age. He was bedridden in the later part of his life and died after a prolonged illness. Bada Baya's mother was also mistreated by her family. They would not give her food and make her hungry for many hours. Kukhia was married off in Bengal. She committed suicide by drowning. She died a dreadful death. None of our neighbour's children studied well. All the children failed and dropped out. They were forced to migrate to other states in search of work. On the other hand, it is a delight to see the families who supported us in our difficult times prosper.

4

Soaring with Hopes and Dreams

Located in one of the farthest corners of Odisha, the primary school in my village was the only educational institution in the area since 1892. There were no middle school or high school in the area. The literacy rate was insignificantly low in the country. Hence, it must have been a very wise man who decided to start a school in my area. When I was five years old, I was enrolled to the school. My first day at school was on Saraswati Puja. My schoolteacher Nilakantha Das took a chalk and, using my fingers, drew the first two Odia alphabets on a slate. My elder sister was also studying in the same school. Along with her, I joined other students in the mid-day feast to celebrate Saraswati Puja. With support and contributions from the students' guardians, the school management committee organized feasts on similar occasions. This was my first time gathering for such an occasion. I was exhilarated to see so many children gathered in one place. Because of our ongoing dispute with the neighbours, I never had a chance to interact or play with children in the village. My first day in school is firmly etched in my mind even today.

The next day, my mother and elder sister tried to teach me the Odia alphabet. Usually, an adult will help a child learn the alphabet by making the child hold a chalk and then draw on a slate. In the process, they would make the child learn and pronounce the drawn alphabet. After repeated trials, the child would learn to draw the alphabet and pronounce it. Normally, the children of the village took a few months to learn the alphabet. However, to everyone's surprise, I learned the alphabet within a few hours of that day. The news spread in the village like wildfire.

Though the school was a few hundred meters from our home, it was not easy to reach. The narrow road to the school passed through the agriculture fields and my elder sister always escorted me to the school. As a result of our ongoing dispute with our neighbours, my parents were apprehensive about my well-being. At no point was I ever left alone, and I grew up under constant vigil. Many days, my mother would be waiting to take me home after school hours; it was not practised by other parents those days. My sister taught me to be watchful and avoid people who looked suspicious and unfamiliar. We hardly went to other houses in the village and did not get the opportunity to know them. I never got the opportunity to explore our village in my early years.

Having nothing to do, I started loving my books. The pictures and beautiful stories enthralled me. I used to be one of the top students in our class year after year. When declaring results, my teachers would proudly declare my marks. Some of the senior students were jealous and surprised by my sharp memory. Once, a senior student made me read a page from his book and repeat it. All my seniors were surprised to see me successfully pass the test.

As mentioned earlier, we always travelled as a family to attend the court cases to the district headquarters. This made our school attendance irregular. The court case and other problems had crippled us financially. In the third standard, my parents sent me to my aunt's place in West Bengal to live for a few months. When I returned home, my teachers came to know and sent a few students to persuade me to join the school again. I was told to appear for the annual examination. Hardly anyone in the village had any ambition to do well academically and aspired to have a career. Children in the village went to school because it was near and they had nothing else to do. My parents were not particularly interested in me joining the school again. I, too, thought that my school days were over. However, due to my teachers' insistence, I appeared for the annual examination and was promoted to the next class. At that time, two new teachers had joined the school. One of them evaluated my mathematics paper and gave me 120 marks out of 100. His argument was that while most of the students performed very poorly on the test, I had attempted one extra question and given all the correct answers. My performance overwhelmed him, so he gave me extra marks. The young teacher believed that I had potential and gave special attention to me in his classes.

Until the 1970s, the government hardly initiated general welfare programmes for economically backward people.

People depended on rain-fed agriculture and practised single crops per year. The farmers did not use fertilizer or pesticides and grew traditional varieties with low yields. The rich people harvested paddy, the staple food for the people in the region. The public distribution system was almost non-existent, and land distribution was skewed in favour of a few rich people. They kept bullocks to cultivate the land and employed bonded labourers for assistance. Hardly anyone kept cows, as there was no market for milk. The poor and young people with no livelihood would enter into an informal agreement with the landlord and work in his house throughout the year for a paltry sum of money and paddy bags. Though the agreement can be termed a form of exploitation, the landlord treated the labourers well. But if the labourer wished to leave or disobeyed the landlord, he would be subjected to severe punishment including beating. Ananta Das was the wealthiest man in our village. His family consisted of three brothers, their wives, and children. Ananta Das's family employed a boy called Kendua. He was a little older than me and brilliant. His father had died at a young age, and to take care of his mother and younger brother, he was forced to work as a bonded labourer. I became Kendua's good friend. His job was feeding the family's bullocks. In the afternoon, he would cook rice husk and feed it to the animals. He was very fond of the bullocks and acted like he was their owner. From him, I learned about bullocks and their characteristics. I, too, developed pride for the animals. Often, I would sit quietly for hours with Kendua while he worked. I would get my story books and read them to him. Kendra, too, would read books in his leisure time. Ananta Das would often find me strolling with Kendua and the bullocks. One day, he asked me if I was still attending school. He also suggested that I should quit school and work at his house. Hearing this, I felt humiliated. Upon returning home, I narrated this to my mother. She gave an earful to Ananta Das and stopped me from meeting Kendua. My friendship with Kendua ended, and I became a lonely boy again.

Droughts, heavy rains, and cyclones were regular features in our area almost yearly. By the end of the monsoon, food and other resources would be scarce. Our school could also not escape the impact as many poor children would drop out. Very few girls studied, as most were married at an early age. The teachers were irregular and would come late. They would come to school at noon, which made the students happy. This meant they could play for longer hours. During the fourth and fifth standards, the school was hardly functioning due to natural calamities in the area. Fortunately, it did not impact my studies. As mentioned earlier, my elder sister was forced to drop out of school. She had to support my parents in household chores. In those difficult times, we could also not afford private tuition for my studies. Many children in the village had tuition masters. I would instead buy the old books from senior students at a discounted rate. All my learning can be attributed to self-study.

The government announced that our primary school would teach till standard seventh. Two new teachers were appointed for this. One of them was Sukhendu Bikash Patnaik. He was a tall, handsome young man who brought a new perspective to the village. As he hailed from a faraway village, he had no option but to live in our village. He converted one of the classrooms into his residential quarter. Sukhendu Bikash Patnaik was a genius. He could not only teach any subject but was also an actor, songwriter, music director, dramatist, and director. His appointment helped the school flourish.

During that time, untouchability was practised rigidly in the school and village. During assembly, children belonging to scheduled castes were made to stand separately. During Ganesh and Saraswati Pujas, they could not come near the deity or touch the prasad. They also abstained from participating in anything related to cooking food or serving it on the grounds of purity. They could eat only after higher-caste children ate their meals. Unlike children of higher caste, they would have to clean their utensils. When the villagers invited the school children and teachers to their houses on festive occasions like marriage, puja, and family functions, discrimination would also be practised. The children from the untouchable community would have to wait till all higher-caste people and their children had finished their meals. No one cared if these children were hungry or reached school late. I reached school late on many occasions. The classes would have begun by then, and everyone would stare at me for coming late. With a false sense of superiority, they would mock me. In those times. I felt humiliated and disgraced, and it had a serious effect on my self-esteem. One day,

I decided to stop going to people's places when they invited schoolchildren. I considered it better to go hungry than to bear any humiliation.

The new teacher came from a better school and a reformed village. He could not tolerate such social segregation and ensured the system was changed. The school environment became democratic. All the students were allowed to participate in all the activities without any discrimination. He ignored the villagers, who showed their reservations about his decision. He stayed with his family on the school premises and took care of the school property. The school pond, garden, coconut trees, and the building were maintained. He introduced the concept of night boarding in the school. The children would contribute money and rice towards their share of the dinner cost in the school. After school hours, the children would return to the school campus in the evening with lanterns, mosquito nets, and bedding. He would teach these children till dinner time, give them tasks, and solve their problems. He introduced English and Hindi in the curriculum. The study hours increased, and so did the learning. He taught me English, grammar, and translation. He was confident that I could do better and outshine many.

Apart from taking care of our studies, he also organized extracurricular activities. We were taken to picnics and took part in dramas. I would get the role of the heroin in his drama because of my ability to memorize lengthy dialogues. With his intervention, primary school reached great heights, and so did my interest in my studies. He helped me develop a strong foundation. The school benefitted from another appointment. Ajit Giri joined our school as the headmaster. He came from a very educated family and was equally liberal and cosmopolitan in his outlook. He gave due attention to the school, and as a result, punctuality, attendance, and discipline improved. The students liked his mathematics classes. I became confident that I could, too, get a respectable job and support my parents once I had finished my studies. While I continued my schooling, my parents and elder sister toiled very hard to earn a living. They never asked me for help. Rather, they felt happy that I was performing well in my studies.

The school in our village was only till the seventh standard. Many students would drop out after the seventh standard. With no one pursuing higher education, none of the villagers were eligible for government or private jobs. Only two villagers had been appointed as teachers in schools outside our village. Those who wished to pursue higher studies were made to attend another school a few kilometres from the village. The students had to travel on foot for more than two hours to attend that school. The journey was tiresome, and it would be more difficult during harsh weather.

A benefactor saved us. He had a small betel leaves business. He built a private high school in the neighbouring village. He invited a few of the unemployed graduates from the area to teach in the school. They did not receive any salary but did not mind. The teachers hoped that after a few years, the government would take over the school, and they would get a salary. This had been the practice so far. In the past, several schools had eventually been taken over by the government. The school started in 1974. It brought great hope to the people in the area as children could attend a school located nearby. When it was time for me to choose a high school for education, I was in two minds. The newly opened school had no experienced teachers, and its matriculation result was very poor. On the other hand, if I went to a far way school, then either I would have to take a hostel or travel every day from home. While I was contemplating my options, one of the teachers from the newly opened school came to me. He persuaded me to join the school. His argument was that it would only take a few minutes to reach the school. Moreover, with our ongoing fight with our neighbours, it would be very dangerous for me to travel long distances to attend school. My parents always apprehended that our hostile neighbours could attack or kill me to take revenge on them. The teacher also argued that students played a significant role in their academic performance. If the student persevered and studied diligently, then they were bound to achieve good results. After listening to him and analysing all the pros and cons, I decided to take admission to the local school.

The teachers in the new school were fresh graduates and untrained. But they were very sincere and wanted to produce good results, which would benefit them as well. The school also provided night boarding. The students contributed to running the mess. A cook was hired to serve dinner to all the boarders and the teachers present. The food served in the mess was a simple affair as the students made a meagre contribution. The students ate puffed rice for breakfast, which they brought from home. At night, the benches and desks were rearranged so the students could use them as beds. The students bought their mattresses, quilts, mosquito nets, and lanterns from home. While the arrangement was not very comfortable, the students hardly complained because they came from poor backgrounds. As the teachers also spent the evenings in the school, the students got free tuition. This helped in improving the pass percentage. The hostel would start functioning only a few months before the half-yearly and annual examinations. Some students living nearby attended evening classes in the school and returned home for the night. It was noticed that the students who attended the evening classes performed better than those who did not.

Many of the teachers in the newly opened school had no alternate source of income. They came from joint families and were expected to contribute to the family income. Moreover, some of them were married and had children of their own. The school management was able to pay them only a small sum from the fees paid by the students. The teachers, however, continued to teach in the school for several years. For some of them, the free meal motivated them to take the evening tuition.

One day, a senior student informed me that Ishwar Chandra Giri, the headmaster, wanted me to meet him. Ishwar Chandra Giri was known to be a very strict headmaster. The moment he entered the school gate, there would be pin-drop silence. He was also the science teacher. He used to beat students mercilessly if they did not study well. Some students had even left the school, unable to bear the punishment. Naturally, I was very scared when I was told to meet him. I thought I must have done something wrong, and because of that, he summoned me. The headmaster was sitting on the school veranda and checking the answer sheets for the recently held half-yearly examination for the eighth standard. Other teachers and senior students were also present. On seeing me, he asked me if I had written the answers myself in my exams. When I gave an affirmative reply confidently, he asked me to explain how my answers matched the textbook line by line. He thought I had cheated in my exams and asked me to repeat the answers. When I gave all the correct answers, he was very much astonished. He told others on the veranda that he had yet to see someone with such a good memory. From that day, I became his favourite student, and he took special care of me.

The headmaster believed that I had the potential to top the board examination. He bought books for me from Cuttack. He made me practice translating from Odia to English. He also made me study several volumes of books written by the renowned teacher Baikunthanath Acharya. I sat with the headmaster for long hours and studied diligently. Within a few months, I mastered the art of translation and could write correct English. I was the only student in the school who won prizes in English essay writing competitions conducted in the area. I also gave complete attention to other subjects.

I could memorize lessons line by line, page by page, chapter by chapter from every book that I needed to study. Before going to bed, I revised all the lessons I studied that day. Ishwar Chandra Giri became my inspiration. He ensured that I did not mix with mischievous students. I studied in his presence, and he made me sleep near his bed. He loved me dearly, and my welfare was foremost on his mind. He became my guardian angel.

From childhood, I loved reading novels and storybooks during my leisure time. It provided me with entertainment. The school did not have a library, but these books were readily available to students. One day, I got a detective novel titled Rakata Ranjita Ratri (A Night of Bloodshed). I was so interested in the book that I kept it open under my study book and read it secretly. However, the headmaster found me out, and suddenly, he snatched away the book and went to his room. A few moments later, Gadadhar, the peon, called me to inform me that the headmaster was crying inconsolably. He thought that I lost interest in my studies and had gone astray. Feeling shattered and out of a sense of betrayal, he began weeping. I went to his room and begged his forgiveness. I assured him I would not read any novels until my examination.

The headmaster encouraged me to study humanities in college. He knew my flair for writing and thought I could become an IAS officer. However, he did not favour my taking a career in engineering or medicine.

While the headmaster devoted his time to the school, a tragedy befell his family. His brother, who financially supported the joint family, passed away. The headmaster now became the sole provider of his large joint family. The remuneration from the school was meagre. As a result, besides cultivating his land, he also started taking tuition classes to earn money. His conditions became so pathetic that students voluntarily worked on his land to help him cultivate crops. He began spending less time in the school. Still, he kept motivating and inspiring me. Without such a great teacher in my life, I would not have been able to dream big.

In high school, I took up quizzing apart from participating in literary competitions like essay writing. In the nearby Jhakjhaki village, a youth club was formed under the leadership of Ranjit Das. The youth club aimed to organize various competitions and promote bright students. Within a few days after joining the school, I learned about an essay writing competition being organized by the club. All the high schools in the block area were expected to participate in the competition. Students from eighth to eleventh standards were eligible for the competition. I went there as a matter of curiosity. I could not imagine competing with students three years older than me. The organizers announced the essay writing topic half an hour before the competition so the students would organize their thoughts. The topic was 'The Role of Newspapers in the Modern Society'. I had never read a newspaper until then, nor did I know about the topic. One of the students had an essay book with him. He lent me the book to read a few minutes before the competition started. I read the book and memorized it. Several students participated in the competition. When the result was declared a month later, I came first to everyone's surprise. This was a big boost to my self-confidence, and I started participating in various literary competitions. I brought several trophies home, and people in the locality started talking about me. My parents were very proud to know about my achievements from their acquaintances.

Our block boasted many schools with reputed teachers and an established alumni network. Until then, no one from my high school had passed with good results. Our school wanted to make a mark, and all hopes were on me. The teachers believed that if the students performed well in the matriculation examination in the state, then the school would become famous, and the government would recognize it. This would enable the teachers to get a regular salary.

We went to Bhograi High School to write our final examination. As the school was several kilometres away, the teachers rented a house for us to stay in. The annual high school examination was conducted under pathetic conditions. Teachers could not be found on invigilation duty. Parents and local guardians gathered near the school premises; some even tried entering the campus by scaling the walls. The question papers were leaked, and teachers prepared answers to give to the students. They, in turn, willingly copied the answers. To give students complete freedom to cheat, the invigilators would even leave the hall briefly. There have also been instances where miscreants announced answers for the benefit of the students from outside boundary walls.

The classrooms would be so noisy that writing the exams in peace would be very difficult. External squads visited schools randomly and only for a few minutes. By evening, the next day's question paper was leaked. Rather than concentrating on their studies, the students would try to buy the leaked question paper. Though I paid no attention to such practices, I was disturbed that the examination procedure had become a farce. That year, newspapers ran stories about leaked question papers in the state, and as a result, the Board of Secondary Examination ordered re-examinations of a few papers.

A month later, we reappeared for a few papers. I had been away from home for seven days. On my way back, I met my father, who broke very sad news. My younger sister had passed away. I was very close to her, and she, too, was very fond of me. She was a sharp girl, and I used to teach her. One day, she returned from school early, complaining of a high temperature. Before my parents could act, she died within a few hours. My parents did not inform me, fearing it would affect my exams. My sister's death had a very traumatic effect on me. To date, I can feel her presence in the house whenever I go to my village.

I hoped to top the board examination or at least be in the top ten. During those days, the board declared the names of the top ten students on the radio and in the newspaper. I was shocked to learn that my name did not appear on the list. One of the teachers went to the board office and found that I had scored 64 and 67 out of 100 on two of my mathematics papers. I could not believe this as I consistently scored a perfect 100 on all the mathematics papers in school. I would have been in the top ten if I had got sixty more marks in both papers. However, no one advised me to apply for recounting or re-evaluation. Though I secured very good marks in the examination and topped the district, the pain of not meeting my expectations haunted me for several years.

5

When It Hurts the Inner Self

The older generation says that our area did not have any role in India's freedom struggle. The chief reason for this was its remoteness. Only one person from our village received a freedom fighter's pension. He was not a respectable person and many doubted if he was part of any movement against the British rule. Some people even joked that when India gained independence, even those charged with heinous crimes were released. Surprisingly, the person's name was included in a list of those who had fought for the country. As he was a crook, people believe that he must have given false evidence to the government, claiming he was a freedom fighter. He had never involved himself in any social and political activities, which further increased our suspicion.

As our village was remotely located, it took many years for any social transformation to reach it. Historically, the power shift to the Marathas and from the Marathas to the British did not have any effect on our village administration at the lowest level. However, the impact of social reforms and development in neighbouring states was felt in our village. During the British rule and even after independence, the police were notorious for their cruelty. Even in the 1970s, people feared the police. As the government did not launch any social welfare programmes, the villagers' dependence on the government was negligible. The new government system took time to reach our village. The village was headed by a headman whose name was Badua. He was from the upper caste and his family held this position for ages. He presided over village meetings, made decisions, and declared punishments for those who broke societal norms. He was supported by people from his caste who were in the majority and other so-called superior men. Women had no representation in this traditional system. When the panchayati raj system was introduced, people got the opportunity to elect their ward members, sarpanch, etc. However, the existing traditional village structure overshadowed the new panchayati raj system. It took many years for the new system took time to be effective.

One of the biggest and demeaning problems our village practised was untouchability. Members of lower caste were prohibited from eating with other members. In shops too, people of lower caste were served tea in separate cups. The eateries had separate seating arrangements and utensils for the untouchables. Even landlords kept separate sets of utensils for food for their lower-caste labourers. The landlord or his family would never touch these utensils, let alone clean them. If someone touched them accidentally, they would take a bath to purify themselves. The labourers would clean their own utensils and the place where they ate. Segregation was strictly followed. During village functions and festivals, the untouchable people would be served food at the end after everyone from the higher caste had eaten.

The untouchables were prohibited from entering temples. Only the upper caste had access to the inner sanctum where the deities were installed. We could not touch the flowers and other offerings for the deities. In many villages, the scheduled caste community could not even wear sandals. In certain places, the untouchables could not wear slippers or hold umbrellas in front of higher-caste members. They had to carry their slippers as a mark of their respect while passing their masters. Similarly, they would have to fold their umbrellas while walking in front of them, even if it was raining heavily. They were not allowed entry into upper-caste homes. In certain areas, they could not use common village paths or access common public properties like wells, ponds, pastures, gochars, and temples. The discrimination did not stop even after their death. The lower-caste people could not cremate their family members in the cremation ground though it was a government land. They were forced to dispose of the dead bodies on the side or some vacant land. The Brahmins did not perform rituals related to departed souls, marriage, puja, etc. Only a particular type of priest would do those functions in the houses of untouchables.

Till the 1970s, our school also followed this discrimination. Bonded labour was also rampantly followed. Youths belonging to lower castes served their masters for a very little sum of money or a few bags of paddy. If any lower-caste person refused to perform his caste duty, the traditional village panchayat would enforce a social boycott or award physical punishment. Then that person and his family members would have a very difficult life. Many times, unable to bear the wrath of the dominant caste, they would leave the village. They would go to a distant village and settle on its outskirts on government land with the consent of the villagers there. Such people were normally assetless and depended on labour work for their survival.

Our village had a cultural troupe, popularly called a kirtan party. Its members used to sing bhajan and kirtans and play music to the beat of mridang. They would go on tours when invited by different villages. They would perform on ceremonial occasions when puja for Shri Chaitanya Mahaprabhu took place. Once, this group of people ate in the house of an untouchable person. When others came to know about this, a meeting was held. It was adjudicated that the young people had lost their caste and to make them regain their original caste and kinship, they had to perform atonement. A special puja was organized and Brahmins were fed. They were also tonsured. When I came across such events, I wanted to revolt against such social norms. While there was no escape route, I was unwilling to accept inferior treatment.

Before India gained independence, Mahatma Gandhi was anguished to witness the practice of untouchability in the country. He spent a considerable period of his life trying to address this social evil. He undertook a historic padayatra in 1934 in Odisha to end untouchability. On several visits to the state, he made efforts for the lower caste to enter the temple. Despite being a staunch Hindu devotee, he never entered the Jagannath Temple in Puri, where the untouchables were prohibited entry. He desired to bring reform in the societal practice by changing the mindset of higher-caste people. He also advised the downtrodden to shun habits that were seen as unclean. On his visit to Delanga in Puri, Mahatma Gandhi said in a public meeting,

> Odisha is the dearest place in India for me. When I reached India, I came to know the poverty, drought of Odisha. I have realised that if I could serve the people of Odisha, I will realise that I have served India. Odisha became a sacred place to me, not because of Lord Jagannath, but because his doors are closed for the Harijans, so it is for me. This is my tirtha, and for this reason I have started to remove the work of the untouchability system from here on my padayatra. I heard that the orthodox people wanted me to be killed and stop the untouchable work. If I go by train or by motor, it is not easy for them to kill me. Apart from this, the pilgrim should go on a walk for pilgrimage. The pilgrim takes the name of the lord, forgets the pain and anguish and offers his service at the feet of the lord while going on pilgrimage by foot. Whether we will backtrack if the sanatani brothers disturb Puri or face them with the policy of non-violence. This is not possible if I move in the train or motor. So, I have decided to walk on foot for the rest of the days of Harijan padayatra.

Gandhiji faced stiff opposition from the so-called sanatanis. The hardliners did not want untouchability to end and threatened his life.

But Mahatma Gandhi was unstoppable. Due to his efforts and those of his followers, by March 1934, three temples in Odisha, namely Raghunathji Temple in Berhampur, Ganjam; Khirochora Gopinath Temple in Remuna, Balasore; and the Siva Temple in Kujang, Jagatsinghpur, opened their doors for everyone. Influenced by his belief, many upper-caste households employed lower-caste people as their domestic servants in Balasore town. A few even accepted food and water from their hands. Many people even dined publicly with the untouchables. But mostly, the movement was confined to urban areas. But when volunteers and congressmen took the initiative to the villages, reforms were seen there, too. Followers of Mahatma Gandhi arranged public dinners in the villages where scheduled caste people were invited to sit and eat with upper-caste Hindus. Bathing ghats and wells were opened for them. The municipal well in Jajpur was opened for the 'untouchables'. All these events were the sign of a new era.

Harekrushna Mahatab, one of the most towering personalities of Odisha, introduced the Orissa Removal of Civil Disabilities Bill on 30 September 1946 in the second session of the assembly. The main purpose was to remove certain disabilities which a certain section of the Hindu community was subjected to till that time. The members of the House unanimously supported the bill. The most important clause of the Bill for removal of civil disabilities was as follows: 'Notwithstanding any law, custom, usage or prescription to the contrary no Hindu shall, by reason merely of his belonging to any particular community or class known as Harijans, "untouchables", Depressed Class or the like be prevented or disabled from being appointed to any public office or enjoying or having access to any public-stream, river, well, tank, pathway, sanitary convenience, or means of transport or any secular institution which the general public belonging to all other classes and communities of Hindus have a right to enjoy or have access to.' This was a kind of social revolution which Mahatma Gandhi fought for throughout his lifetime. This legislation was welcomed widely.

The Orissa Temple Entry Authorisation and Indemnity Bill 1947 was introduced in the House on 14 February 1947 to remove inequality in the untouchable community. However, the bill was primarily objected to by the opposition leader and the deputy leader. With the persuasion of other leaders, both these politicians withdrew their objections. The bill was passed on 14 February 1947. It was submitted for the assent of the governor-general. On receipt of assent on 9 April 1947, the legislation came into force. So, in this way, the then Ministry adopted two important legislative measures for uplifting the condition of the lower-caste people, especially their social status. The Orissa Debt Bondage Abolition Regulations, 1948 came into force via law department notification on 17 June 1948 to abolish the system of debt bondage. The gothi (bonded labour) was abolished and actions were taken to abolish beth begari. The Orissa Moneylenders Bill, 1947, was adopted by the Orissa Legislative Assembly on 10 March 1947. It was another milestone to check slavery.

While the legal system was being reformed and urban India was changing, rural India was still holding to the age-old regressive traditions. In rural areas, people remained ignorant and continued to follow the social evil of the caste system. Zamindars continued to follow this system as it suited their convenience and enabled them to dominate and economically oppress the poor. Till the 1980s, my village rampantly followed untouchability. The social changes that Mahatma Gandhi envisaged were not visible. People who supported the caste system and other social evils spoke ill about Mahatma Gandhi. The adoption of the Constitution of India also did not bring any major changes at the ground level. After Mahatma Gandhi's assassination, people did not voice this issue or work as seriously as he would have liked. In comparison to Odisha, the neighbouring state of West Bengal was fast becoming egalitarian. The lower caste were asserting their rights, backed by the new legal system. As our village was located near the Bengal border and marital exchanges were common, we, too, were exposed to the social changes taking place in the neighbouring state. But the changes took time to usher in our area.

The way we were treated as human beings was inhuman. Even while growing up, we were confronted with caste barriers in school and other social gatherings. Even if lower-caste communities were invited to social occasions organized by higher-caste people, they were not received with dignity. They would be made to sit separately and on bare ground. Sometimes, one has to be satisfied with sitting on a moist ground. They could not touch higher-caste people. If a lower-caste person sat on the same mattress as the higher-caste person, it would mean that their bodies had touched, thereby the higher-caste person becoming impure. The lower-caste people could not use the same wells and ponds as used by the higher-caste community. In social gatherings, the lower-caste people could eat only after the upper caste had been served food. After the lower caste finished their meals, the place would be cleaned with cow dung and water as a measure of purification. When serving food, it would be dropped on the plate to prevent accidental contact. A lower-caste man could eat in the house of upper-caste people; He would be made to sit on the ground below the verandah of the house. But the upper-caste man would never eat in a lower-caste household. They would not even drink water in the houses of the less privileged. As a child, I would often wonder what made the water in our house impure for them.

Many Hindu customs and rituals require the presence of people from the lower caste. On such grounds, our forefathers from Bengal had been made to settle on a piece of land on one extreme corner of the village. Over the years, a hamlet developed. Later, our forefathers purchased land from other villagers. However, the upper-caste communities controlled the entire government land in the area and slowly became legal owners of it. The revenue department regularized all the government land in their favour. In contrast, the poor and lower-caste communities were barred from encroaching on any government land. One can only imagine the pathetic conditions under which my ancestors lived. The agrarian system in rural areas was a major cause of bonded labour, and the caste system created unequal opportunities for the poor and the rich.

At the centre of our village stands a temple dedicated to Goddesses Shitala and Manasa. The village elders had built it many decades ago. Every year, an annual puja was held in the temple and people made donations for the celebrations. A few were responsible for managing the temple and performing various rituals. This group of people had been in control since the time of the temple's construction. Besides the annual puja, offerings were made on a daily basis for which priests had been appointed. The priests and their families lived in the land recorded in the deities' names. The lower-caste people had no role in the affairs of the temple. They could not even step inside the temple premises and offered their prayers only from a distance.

Once, when I was a child, I went to the temple with some village boys. I was playing some games on the village street with them. The priest had left the temple after the morning puja. The boys entered the temple and paid their offerings inside the sanctum sanctorum. On their invitation, I, too, went inside and prostrated before the deity. However, after a few days, everyone came to know that I had entered the temple and as a result, the priests and many villagers revolted.

The priests performed rituals to purify the deities and temple, and my parents had to face a difficult time on account of my innocent act.

I was a bright child and punctual in attending school and doing my homework. Every student was expected to complete their homework or would face the teacher's wrath. The teachers wanted all the students to do their tasks so that they could be recorded, and on inspection by the authorities, the teachers did not face any trouble. The teaching in the school was quite poor, and hence, many students faced difficulty in understanding the lessons and completing their homework. Their parents were also busy and could not help their wards. Some students were assisted by their tuition teachers. The schoolteachers were not concerned if the finished assignments had been copied from another student. When a student failed to finish their assignment, they met very harsh punishment. The teachers would beat them mercilessly with a cane stick. The students would have deep-cut marks on their hands, backs, legs, and other body parts. It was a traumatic experience for those who met such a fate. Many of the students who were regularly punished would start skipping school and instead hide in paddy fields, forests, and bushes during school hours. They would return home only when the school closed, and their parents would think that their children were attending school regularly.

A few of my classmates would come to my house early in the morning every day. They would sit on our verandah and copy the assignment from my notebook. To keep me in good humour, they would give me chocolate, mango, or something to eat. My close friend was Ananta. He visited my house regularly and copied my assignments. For safety reasons, I could not go to his house. We would go to school together. After the school got over, he would come to my house. One day, a villager saw us eating from the same plate. He told this to the upper-caste people in the village. Ananta's kins and neighbours felt that a significant violation had been committed, and Ananta should atone for it by performing some rituals. However, his father did not agree. He believed his son had not committed any crime. The villagers excommunicated his family for several months but he stayed firm on his decision. The matter got cooled only with the passage of time.

For more than eight decades since the inception of the school, segregation of lower-caste students was a matter of practice. The caste rule on purity was very much visible and strictly enforced. The students would be segregated and seated separately in class and during prayers. The untouchable students were kept away from non-academic activities, where the teachers needed the involvement of students. The impression I got was that other students had superior rights in the school compared to us. The worst things to be observed was at the time of puja and feast in the school when lower-caste students were unwanted and treated in the most inhuman manner. Since it was enforced in the school, it almost got sanctified as a rule. The children would practice these principles at home as they grew up.

I became friends with a Brahmin boy. One day, he took me to his house, and I sat on a cot on the verandah. His mother was making a pan and kept the betel leaf and other ingredients on the cot. She could not tell me on my face that I had broken a rule by sitting on her cot. After I left and was some distance away, I heard her shouting, 'That boy sat on the cot and now everything has become impure.' I felt I was slapped hard that day, and I never played with the boy again.

To earn a living, my mother worked in a rich man's house. During paddy harvest, men and women would go in groups with their sickles and cut the paddy in his field. The rich man would pay the workers their daily wage and serve two meals: breakfast and lunch. As during harvest time my school will be closed, I would join my mother in the field. The allurement was the free meal and wage. As my output was low, the landlord would only give me a free lunch at noon and no wage. All the workers would be seated in a line and food would be served by the women of the house. These women treated the workers like slaves. They would throw food on our plates in such a manner that it would spoil our dresses. We had no option but to tolerate this disgusting behaviour.

My high school was two kilometres from my house. A schoolteacher lived on the way. The custom in those days was that when a child was born, its clothes be washed by someone from my caste. The schoolteacher had a newborn. He did not want to employ an adult to do this job. Instead, he would keep a vigil and catch me on my way back home. He would force me to wash the so-called impure clothes.

However hard I tried to avoid him, he would catch hold of me. I found this very demeaning and could never respect him in my life.

As a child, every cell of my body revolted against caste discrimination. The system tried to tell me that I was inferior to the rest of the world. But by no means was I inferior to anyone. I was far better in my studies and extracurricular activities than my friends. Instead of being appreciated, I was made to feel low and inferior because of these practices.

My classmates would also play the caste card when they could not compete with me. It was a practice for the senior students of Regional Engineering College, Rourkela, to welcome freshers from their alma maters by hosting a dinner. Three of us from Fakir Mohan College took admission in Regional Engineering College, Rourkela, in 1985. I came to know from sources that two of my classmates attended the dinner organized by senior students. A few months later, one of the senior students visited our hostel. He was surprised to know that I, too, was his alma mater. He asked one of my classmates why I had not been invited for dinner. My classmates told it was because I was from a scheduled caste community. While the senior student did not like my classmate's comment, I was astonished to know my classmate harboured such feelings. My classmate scored lower marks than me in all the examinations. Years later, during the COVID-19 outbreak, he was affected very severely. His family contacted me for assistance, and with much difficulty, I was able to arrange a bed for him at the peak of the infection. I ensured that he got the best of treatments but unfortunately, he succumbed to the dreaded disease. I helped his family get reimbursement and a job for his wife under the company's rehabilitation assistance scheme.

Old customs and traditions took time to change in our village. In 1998, my parents invited all the villagers to join us for my marriage feast. But the gram rakshi played havoc. At the behest of the upper caste, he questioned how we dared to invite the higher caste for a feast. I realized that even if I became an Indian administrative officer, the upper-caste community in my village would still discriminate against us. The matter went to such a pass that I sought the help of the superintendent of police to act against one of the villagers who worked in the police department.

Every time I visited my village, the villagers would remind me that I was born in a lower caste. It gave me a lot of mental stress and pain. I felt I was worth nothing despite all the achievements I had accomplished.

The mental stress I was subjected to as a child was on account of the practice of untouchability by the villagers. It was a caste-based practice and included several forms of social ostracism and exclusion that were based on the ideas of purity, pollution, hierarchy, and subordination.

Article 17 of the Constitution prohibits the practice of untouchability. It makes clear that not only the caste-based practice of untouchability is constitutionally prohibited, but all such practices bear a resemblance to it. Unfortunately, it took time for this rule to reach my village resulting in social subordination, exclusion, and segregation even after several decades of adopting the Indian constitution.

6

Poverty That Ruined the Backbone

As my village was remotely located, it had very little exposure to the outside world. Only a few people had radio sets and there were no newspapers. The only newspaper that the village received was subscribed to by the primary school and was a minimum of fifteen days old. The only school in the village taught till the fifth standard. If anyone wished to opt for higher studies, they were considered too adventurous. The people in my village had no aspirations. Such a traditional society with limited resources always tries to survive on its own, adjusting to the scarcities and shortages. A few young men dared to travel to Kolkata and other places in West Bengal in search of work. Digha, the nearest tourist town on the seashore, was yet to be developed. Only a few temporary shops were there to meet the requirements of casual visitors.

People in our village with land were considered wealthy and powerful. Money lending and mortgaging were common. Children of rich families were sent to schools while the poor looked for wage employment in the village. The poor believed that attending school was of not much benefit to them. A dismal number of girls went to school and most were married at a young age. Initiatives such as mid-day meals had not been started in schools, which would have attracted children from poor communities to take admission. Neither free books nor uniforms were distributed, nor were any scholarships or stipends given. If the government provided any such assistance, they were misused by the officials. The teachers believed in awarding physical punishment to the students for not doing well in the classes. But they never dared to punish children from rich families. They were treated with far more politeness. In contrast, children from poor families were subjected to brutal punishments. Such practice led to further low school attendance and dropouts.

When my parents were busy fighting cases, our lands remained fallow. The family's only source of income was from wage labour. My father would leave early for work before I or my siblings woke up. He would sleep only for a few hours. Normally, he worked in the betel leaf vines and returned late in the night. Every week, haat bazaars would be held near our village in four to five locations on different days. Haats are open-air markets that serve as trading venues for local people in rural areas. On such days, my father would return home even later than usual. He would go to these markets to buy essential items and return a little before midnight. Me and my sisters would be fast asleep by the time my father would return home. Dinner would be cooked from the things my father bought from the markets. It would usually be rice, vegetables, and other things. My mother would wake me up and feed me with great affection. I was allowed to sleep only after I had my food. However, there were days when we had nothing to eat in the morning. Some days the landlord would send puffed rice. For many years, I believed the landlord was a generous person who understood our difficulties. It was only much later that I came to know that it was my father who sent the puffed rice which the landlord gave him to eat in the morning. My father would remain hungry to save his children from hunger. I know I can never repay him for his sacrifices.

The wage my father earned was meagre. It was not enough to meet ends. We could not buy clothes regularly and the ones we bought would be the cheapest. I had only one pair of dresses for school. We had no woollen clothes. During winter, my mother would wrap her old sarees around me to save me from biting cold. To protect us from severe winter, we would make quilts of a thick mat made of straw and cover it with a thin cloth. Early in the mornings, my father would collect dried leaves and burn them. We would sit before the fire till it was daytime. My mother could not buy new sarees and wore the old ones. However, she had a silk saree from her happier and better-off days. She would make it a point to visit her father's house two to three times a year. When jackfruits and pineapples grew in our garden, she would pack and carry them to her father's house every summer. She visited her parent's house thrice a year. To reach her village, we had to cross a coast canal constructed during the Victorian era. Just before reaching her destination, she would take out her precious saree, gold necklace, earrings, and other ornaments and put them on. These were the only possessions she was left with after the family had sold everything. She wanted to look good and did not want anyone from her village to blame her father for her poor conditions. There were days when my father would fall sick and could not go out for work. The scarcity would be felt in the kitchen and I would pray to god for his early recovery so that our sufferings lessened.

We were lucky that we had coconut trees, jackfruit trees, and pineapple bushes on our homestead land. Our horticulture produce supplemented our meagre family income. My father could climb coconut trees and was employed by other villagers to climb their trees. It was one of his sources of income. The slender trees could be more than 30 feet tall, and I would constantly fear that he may accidentally fall. I would pray to god to protect him.

My father would sell our horticulture produce in the weekly market to augment the family income. I would accompany him sometimes. It took hours for the produce to get sold. He would sit with abundant patience while I would become restless after some time. On rainy days and during winter, the sales would be low. Some days, the sale would continue till very late in the night. He would offer a heavy discount and dispose of the remaining ones as the last recourse. Even though we wanted to eat the jackfruits or pineapples from our garden, they would be sold instead. With the money my father would buy rice, necessary for our survival. Coconuts, jackfruit, and pineapples were luxury for us.

My mother also contributed to the family income. The children were growing up, which meant more food was required. She had learnt to weave fishing nets. In her leisure time, she would weave one. After two to three months, a cast net would be ready. She would give the profit she earned by selling the nets to my father. Both understood each other very well.

Another skill she had learnt was making ropes from coconut fibre. She would collect coconut husks, dry them, and manually take out the coir fibre. After cleaning and removing the short fibres, she would roll the ropes. Many houses needed such ropes for construction, agricultural activities, and betel leaf vines. Even if she got tired or blisters would appear on her hand, she did not give up. She had perfected this art and could make ropes for various purposes. One day, the local MLA came to our house and informed his wish to set up a rope-making factory in the area. My mother rejoiced to hear this as it meant she could get regular employment. But the factory remained a wish.

Each day my mother would think of new ideas to earn money. She would go to the Deula market, which was 5 kilometres away, to buy paddy at a relatively better rate. She could carry a maximum of 50 kilograms of paddy on her head on each trip and, on some days, made three to four trips to that market. Each trip would take 3 hours on foot. On returning home, she would boil paddy with water, dry it in an open area under the sun, and take it to the local rice huller. My elder sister would assist her. On certain days, I would accompany her and carry 10 kilograms. I would often dream of growing big and strong so that I could carry more quantities of paddy and give respite to my mother.

My mother prepared two types of rice. One for simple cooking and the other for making puffed rice. Some people came to the house to buy the rice. Other times, my mother would go to the nearby market on Tuesdays to sell the rice. I would accompany her on such trips as she needed my help in matters of money. She knew I made the correct calculation. Every time she made a profit. As a child, I would observe how people conducted business in the market. People who were smart and young disposed of their stock quicker than others. They used sweet talk and friendly manners to attract customers. Our rice would be of better quality than others, but my mother took a longer time to sell it. She would sit with her rice stock with tremendous patience and never showed any irritation. At late hours, my father would come to the market, and we would return home with unsold rice stock. I never saw my mother being frustrated. She had no complaints about her life.

My mother and I would reach the market much before the buyers arrived. The shopkeepers would still be busy setting up their shops and stalls. In those days, the marketplace was a vast open field with few permanent structures. The shopkeepers had designated places where they erected temporary structures using bamboo poles and polythene sheets. After noon, when the sun was not hot and bright, people would trickle in. At the peak of our poverty, we would bring home the stale and rotten vegetables and fruits that the shopkeepers had thrown away. We had no money to buy fresh vegetables. My mother would cut away the rotten portions of the vegetables and cook only the good parts. I could hear her weeping softly while cooking. The cooked curry would be pungent to smell. Sometimes, we did not even have this pungent curry but only rice to eat. Living in such dire conditions was very painful, and I was not sure if we would ever get to see better days.

On one of our trips to the market, we were late. The market was still a few miles away, and we were walking briskly. It was afternoon, and midway, a barren stretch of land would come. The land was sandy and lined with tall palm trees. Fleets of birds could be seen in the azure sky. I was very excited to go to the market, as I had a few things to buy.

However, suddenly, a gust of cool breeze from the east blew the sand all over. Before we could comprehend anything, bright flashes of light struck the sky. The lightening shattered the earth and was followed by loud thunder and shock waves. It had struck a tall tree, and fumes billowed from it. We were awestruck, and I lost consciousness.

I regained my senses an hour later. When I opened my eyes to the soft call of my mother, I saw her kind face looking at me. She looked calm, with no fear or pain. She had carried me to the nearest habitation in her not-so-strong arms. The strength I saw in her comfiture that day still baffles me. This is the reason I remember the incident so vividly.

I was barely ten years old when another life-shattering event hit us. The weekly market was particularly crowded that day. It was late afternoon and the sun was setting in. My mother was bargaining with a rice seller for a better price. I was standing next to her. It was so noisy that my mother's voice was hardly audible. Suddenly, there was a commotion and people were running helter-skelter. Within a few seconds, somebody threw me away. When I got up, I saw my mother lying on the ground, shouting for me. Blood was oozing from one of her legs. A stray bull had run amok on the crowd and hit my mother. It fractured her leg. People tried to help her and covered her wounded leg with a jute bag. I was transfixed, not knowing what to do. Then it occurred to me that I should find my father, who had also accompanied us that day. Before I could do so, he had already reached the accident site. With the help of fellow villagers, my father carried her to the local hospital in a palanquin. I could hear her scream when the doctor on duty operated on her and put a plaster without anaesthesia. I prayed that she would get well. I knew that without her our life had no meaning. Incidentally, it was the same hospital where she breathed her last many years later.

She remained in the hospital for fifteen days. The hospital was located in a remote area and had no facility for the attendants to stay. My father and I used to spend the night in the hospital while my elder sister would stay during the daytime. The hospital room was infested with mosquitoes, and to escape them, I and my father would sleep under my mother's bed by tying a mosquito net on the four legs of the bed made of aluminium. Her entire leg was plastered and we were doubtful if she would ever walk again.

We returned home, and after three months, it was my mother who removed the plaster using a sharp blade. However, her leg had stiffened and she could not walk. My elder sister went to the doctor and took his advice. He told her that my mom needed to do physiotherapy exercises at home. My mother took the advice seriously and did the exercises diligently. To our great satisfaction, she was able to walk after six months. To pay her gratitude, she went to meet Dr Sahu, who had saved her leg and performed the difficult operation. She was still finding it too difficult to walk, but nevertheless, she went to meet him in the hospital. She took coconuts and other fruits from our garden as presents. I always saw the doctor as a messiah. When I went to study in Balasore, I paid him a visit to express my gratitude. He remembered me and the dreadful night when he had to perform a difficult operation on my mother without proper medical support.

My mother tried her luck in cultivating betel leaves. One of our plots was suitable for cultivating betel leaves and was lying fallow. After levelling the sandhill and clearing the forest growth, she erected the required structure with the support of my father and sister. My father went to Mohanpur in West Bengal to buy good planting materials. My mother spent a lot of time and energy on the betel vine and took my elder sister's help. Betel plants need a lot of care. It needs to be irrigated every second day. My mother would fill large earthen pitchers from a nearby small pond and carry them to water the betel leaf vine. It was a very laborious process and took many hours to complete. Everything had to be done manually as motorized pumps had not yet come into the area. My sister helped my mother in watering the betel vines. When the plants grow tall, the leaves at the lower end of the creeper have to be plucked. This leafless lower end is then covered with sand and buried underground. To do this, the creepers are lowered from the support sticks and tied again to the sticks with a particular type of thread made from grass. It is a laborious and cumbersome task which needs to be done sitting, positing, and moving forward from one plant to another. Sand has to be carried inside the vine to bury the creepers beneath. My mother worked very hard and hoped the cash crop would give her a good return as it did for other rich people in our village. However, she lacked experience and expertise and the betel leaves produced were smaller in size. It was also attacked by pests. As a result, she got lower returns than her expectations. Her efforts were not entirely successful. Our neighbours lost no opportunity to taunt her and said that cultivating betel leaf vine was not a woman's job.

After Gadadhar Pal deceitfully took away two of our plots, my father refused to cultivate the remaining ones. He thought it would be better to keep the rest of the land fallow, or else his case would get weakened. He was protesting against the injustice meted out to him. However, my mother decided to cultivate the land adjacent to our house to supplement the family income. We had no bullocks or plough. In those days, cultivation was done with the help of draught animals.

She employed an agricultural hoe fixed to a wooden handle to till the land. She grew seedlings and transplanted the paddy crop. She had only hand tools to do the cultivation, which made the task tedious and painful. However, she did not give up. With a great deal of energy, she cultivated the plot of land and grew paddy to support the family.

When life would become unbearable, she would take us to her father's village. Her father earned well from agriculture. Normally, the relatives would be nice to us. But one time, we had overstayed our welcome, and as a result, my grandfather and others behaved rudely with us. Unable to bear their rude behaviour, she left her father's house abruptly. Since then, she would visit her father's house only when her presence was required for ceremonial occasions. She learnt a hard lesson that even one's blood relations desert us at the time of crisis. I would often wonder why our relatives who were well off could not stand by us during our hard times. My parents never asked for help.

One day my mother's brother visited our house on a rainy day. He knew that my mother had some golden ornaments and asked for them. He wanted to mortgage those to a money lender for a loan to start a business. Surprisingly, he did not think of mortgaging his wife's ornaments. For the first time, my mother made a tough decision and refused to part away with her precious possessions. My maternal uncle got livid and immediately left the house. In his wildest dream, he did not think his sister would refuse him. Years later, my mother sold those bangles when money was required for my education.

Odisha and West Bengal have been deeply influenced by the teachings of Chaitanya Mahaprabhu. He is well known for introducing the Bhakti movement in Odisha. Influenced by his teachings, many people adopted Vaishnavism in our area. To become a Vaishnav, one does not need to be born in any particular caste. People are indoctrinated into the sect and have to follow a particular lifestyle and chant the maha-mantra. There are many mutts that worship Chaitanya Mahaprabhu. On special days, people take out his idols. A mahotsav is also organized when someone's wishes are fulfilled. During the puja, kirtan is performed in front of the deities. The ceremony can last several days. Our village had a kirtan troupe. Many young men were its members. They sang kirtans and bhajans and played the mridang, cymbals, and other musical instruments. They would dance for hours. Various villages would invite the team to perform. They would be paid in cash and kind. They would get free food and clothes. However, the troupe members were Vaishnavs and performed kirtan as a matter of faith and not to earn a living. The troupe was respected by all for their spirituality. The troupe enacted a play titled 'Nimain Sanyas'. The play was in Bengali, and it was about the life of Chaitanya Mahaprabhu and his brother from Nabadweep.

My elder sister was a talented singer. Spotting her talent, the members asked her to join the kirtan party and play the role of Shri Chaitanya. She was hardly ten years old but travelled with the team for performance. I, too, accompanied her on several occasions and was mesmerized by her performance on stage. We went with the team whenever there was a call. I was too small to play the mridang and participate in kirtan and therefore took part in singing chorus with the team. Chanting 'Hare Krishna' with hundreds of people gave rise to a unique feeling. There was a time when I thought of leaving my studies and joining the kirtan troupe permanently. When I expressed my desire to the troupe leader, he disagreed and said I should continue my studies.

My elder sister was also a very brilliant student. But our family circumstances forced her to leave school. After completing the fifth standard, she worked with the kirtan troupe for a few years in lieu of a small income.

Two more classes were added to the primary school, namely sixth and seventh standards. However, the government did not make any provision for supporting infrastructure. Already, the school was struggling to conduct all five classes. Five classes were adjusted in three rooms. One-half of a room was used by teachers as an office. To accommodate the additional classes, the villagers constructed a semi-permanent structure made of mud and thatched roof. It had three rooms. The teachers went to the village and asked the parents to admit their wards to the new classes. My sister, too, retook admission to the school. The government gave monetary incentives to the likes of her. However, she dropped out of seventh standard and could not pursue further studies. Keeping with the prevailing village customs, my parents got her married at a very young age. My younger sister dropped out of school after my elder sister was married. She was needed for household work. I, on the other hand, was lucky to be allowed to study without interruption. Had my sisters been given the same opportunities I got, their lives would have been different.

If life was not already hard, cyclones and torrential rains made it harder. Our area was prone to natural disasters. During that time, the government did not warn us about the impending disasters. In the 1970s, we were hit by cyclones a number of times. Each time, the disaster caused untold destruction. Not only our houses were damaged, but so would be our livelihood. The people were dependent on betel leaf cultivation. Restoration would cost money, and at that time, the government did not provide any monetary relief to the affected people. The banks were non-existent at that time and only village money lenders provided loans. The daily wage workers would be the hardest hit. I remember the painful days of hunger and semi-famished conditions following a natural calamity, though my parents did their best to protect us. In one such incident following a cyclone in our area, the village remained totally cut off from the rest of the state for a few days. The food stock in our house got over and we were forced to remain hungry. I still cannot forget the hunger and the associated pain of that day. We were saved when a gentleman named Faku Behera from our village came to our house with half a kilogram of wheat. My mother made porridge from it to stop us from crying. I am indebted to him even to this day. The miseries continued for several months that year. Our school building was completely damaged. It took months to repair it. When the school reopened, many students from poor families had dropped out. Girls had been married off to lessen the pressure on the families.

The betel vine owners followed a peculiar practice in those days; they did not allow female workers on their farms. The owners were rich and did not need the women of their households to go to the market or work in the field. It was considered a matter of social prestige that their women were kept inside the house. The labour market was male-dominated. The only deviation was seen in the case of poor families. Deprived of employment opportunities in betel vines, my mother would join other labourers of the village in various operations related to paddy cultivation. She helped in transplanting, paddy cutting, transporting paddy stock to the threshing floor, and in threshing operations. The employment was seasonal. During the winter vacation, I worked with my mother in paddy fields. Except for Faku Behera, who recognized my worth and paid some wages, the other landlords considered my output low, and I had to be satisfied only with free food.

Before I finished high school, my elder sister got married, which caused me a lot of grief. When my mother was out for work, my sister took care of me. My younger sister, too, met a similar fate a few years later. When I went for higher studies, the pressure on my parents to earn additional income was reduced. Their lives became easier.

The chief cause of our misery and suffering was the land dispute with Radhakrishna Pal and his family. As the dispute ran over a few decades, we were progressively ruined. Though there was no less affection in the family, the prospects of getting justice from the court kept my parents on tenterhooks. This would often lead to marital discord between my parents; my mother would blame my father for all the misfortunes. On those painful days and nights, I would pray to god to deliver us from this misfortune. I would promise myself to study hard and become a successful person.

7

Inspired by Pure Love and Promises

Our survival in the village was no less than a miracle. My parents struggled to provide for our family and protect us from the new challenges that arose every day. The situation grew more complex and dangerous by the day, with our neighbours constantly putting pressure on us to leave the village. Our house was located on a large piece of land, surrounded by their houses and separated by easily passable boundaries. The front gate leading to our property remained tightly closed for several years. Only a few villagers came to check on us from time to time, entering through the northern back side of the property. They provided us with some assistance and kept us informed about events on the other side. Our lives were at the mercy of the almighty. My parents feared what they could do if our enemies attacked us in the middle of the night when we were asleep and defenceless.

Though there were certain minor disputes earlier, the trouble intensified a few years following my birth. Till that time, my parents had not sold away their land and all other properties. Till the 1970s, our area was in a very backward territory, and there were no medical facilities in the rural area.

The kids born to my young mother were dying one by one. On that score, she was subjected to torment and verbal abuse by the women of the neighbourhood. A person advised her to visit the nearby Chandaneswar Temple for worship and prayers. The holy shrine of Lord Shiva is an important religious centre not only for the people of Odisha and West Bengal but also for people from many other parts of India. Although the temple is visited by large numbers of people on a daily basis, the unique sight during the Chadak mela for a darshan of the lord is a wonderful experience. The exact history associated with the holy temple is not known, but it is often popularly believed that the shrine originated on its own. Since then, it has been developed into a temple and is worshipped by a large number of devotees. Every year, a grand fair is held at the temple on the first day of the Odia calendar. The fair attracts many devotees who come to visit the temple. It is believed that fasting for several days during this time can fulfil one's wishes. One day, without informing my father, my mother left the house and went to the temple. Lord Chandaneswar is highly revered in the area, and it is said that anyone who visits the temple and lies down with full devotion, forsaking food, will be granted a boon by Lord Shiva. Even today, many men, women, and children can be seen lying in such conditions within the temple campus. My mother stayed in the temple for several days, accompanied by other devotees, and survived only on the panchamruta (the holy potion) provided by the temple priest. One night, my mother had a dream where Lord Shiva was talking to another god. They were discussing a child who was pointing to my mother and saying that the child belonged to her. The next morning, she happily narrated the scene to the priest. He advised her to return home as he believed her prayer had been granted. My father brought her back home. She had become very frail. To their surprise, I was born within a year. The neighbours who used to accuse her of being unable to bear a son were proven wrong. The family was happy again. After a few days, my father went to the Vishnupad Temple in Gaya, Bihar, to offer pinda, a special type of puja for his parents and other departed blood relatives. When he returned, a priest from the Jagannath Temple came to our village. After seeing the child and discussing it with my parents, he suggested a name for me. Thus, I became known as Bishnupada. Being a male child, I received preferential treatment in the family.

My mother was a devout follower of Lord Chandaneswar until her last breath. Every Monday, she would walk several kilometres to the temple, carrying a green coconut, the leaves of a stone apple tree, and flowers to offer to the Lord. Her only wish was for my well-being and long life. She performed this ritual until she was no longer physically capable of doing so, which coincided with my qualification for the Indian Administrative Service.

The Chadak mela is celebrated at the Chandaneswar Temple every year in the month of Chaitra from 14 March to 14 April. The puja continues for thirteen days, starting with the thirteenth arghya (prayer) to the first arghya. During this time, devotees from all over the country come to make various wishes and accept a sacred thread called paita. The number of devotees increases from the fifth arghya to the third Arghya. They offer their arghyas (prayer) at night. The devotees fast the whole day. On the fourth arghya, a day called 'Kamina Vivah', the marriage of Lord Siva with Kamina, the daughter of the demon Nila, is celebrated. On the second arghya day, 'Nila Parba' is observed, and on the first arghya day, 'Paat Parbha' is celebrated. For some devotees, as per their rigorous manasik (wish), they prick their bodies and tongues with iron nails. The whole gathering is controlled by the Paata Bhakta, the chief devotee. After the Paata Parba, the devotees remove their paitas (sacred thread) after their last arghya and wash it away in the sea. After my birth, my mother had kept some vows to be observed by me at the Chandaneswar Temple, which included accepting the sacred thread and keeping fast. When she felt that I would not be able to perform those rituals, she took those austere practices at her advanced age herself. She had unshakable faith in Baba Chandaneswar.

As a child, observing and facing the difficulties, I swore to take revenge and protect my family from the hostile neighbours when I grew up. I wanted to become a strong man to protect my parents. We did not eat meat at home. My friends who ate meat were stronger and better at sports. I wanted to eat meat to gain strength, so my mother allowed me to eat meat curry at school feasts on special occasions. When my father found out, we had an argument but my mother convinced him. She herself never ate meat or eggs as she followed Vaishnav dharma, like my father. She wanted me to eat meat to become strong. Whenever we went to the nearby weekly market, I would ask her to buy me meat curry and she would stand by my side until I finished, observing with great satisfaction.

My father was very strict when it came to religious beliefs. He was a tough man who could endure a lot of pain. He had a philosophical approach to life and would attribute all his sufferings to the will of God. He had an in-depth knowledge of various principles and stories related to Hinduism. Every night, I would sleep by his side on a small cot and we would accidentally bump into each other. Despite being very tired, I would ask him to tell me a story every night and he would either start a new one or continue from the previous night's tale. If he repeated any story, I would remind him. He would spend the day thinking about what story to tell me, knowing how much I enjoyed them. As a child, I had no idea what my father had gone through during the day or whether he was in the right frame of mind to stay awake, speak, and answer my questions.

The stories would always start with 'once upon a time', 'it was some years ago', or 'in a hamlet there lived', featuring different characters and descriptions of people and places. Although the setting and characters looked familiar, they would often change, leading my young mind from the known reality to an imaginary world of kings, queens, magicians, and fairies. The themes of the stories revolved around the lives of common people, their beliefs, morals, values, and situations. Sometimes, the story portrayed the struggles of good people against cruel ones, while other times a single man would rise against the system. With the support of unseen powers, their epic struggles and miraculous survival would ultimately lead to victory.

My father knew how long to narrate the stories and when to stop. He remembered where he left off the previous night, depending on how soon I fell asleep. He never showed any irritation or anger, even when it was too taxing for him to speak after a long day of hard work without any rest. He kept narrating the stories as long as I stayed awoke.

Running his loving fingers upon my forehead and caressing my hair, he would end with a reassuring message that would bring me a sense of comfort and relief before I drifted off to sleep. He would say things like 'the demon died', 'the poor man had his victory', 'the king granted the boon', or 'God listened to the prayers', something that I could feel good about and that would fill me with wonders as I slept.

Most of my father's stories were about the hardships we faced in the village due to our enemies. These stories instilled in me the courage to do something substantial when I grew up.

My mother was a practical person who understood the value of nutrition for our family. To ensure that we received a regular supply of eggs and milk, she started keeping hens and wanted to buy a cow. Despite my father's objections, she saved money and went to several villages in search of a cow. Finally, she was persuaded to buy a heifer, with the assurance that it would eventually turn into a milch cow. We kept the heifer for over two years, hoping that it would get pregnant and produce a calf. Sadly, it turned out that the heifer was infertile, and my mother's dream of having a milk-producing cow was never realized. At that time, there was no processed milk available in the market and there was veterinary treatment available to treat the infertility problem of the heifer.

For several years, I spent my entire time with her. I went with her to the market, the courts, and to her relatives' houses. I used to miss classes on these grounds. I learnt about the places, stories, and facts from her. Our poverty became enormous and like a mountain. She was always trying to do something to support the family.

She used to narrate the events of the court to the children. We learned that a powerful officer called a collector was in charge of the district, and justice could be delivered if he desired so. Initially, our case was heard by a sub-divisional magistrate who was subordinate to the collector before the criminal procedure code was amended in 1973. The case was adjourned several times and the appeal and revision cases prolonged the dispute. It took almost three decades for the matter to be closed. My mother believed that if the collector had wanted, the same could have been done in a few days. However, she could never hope to see the collector. On each hearing day, all of us would travel to Balasore katcheri and sit near the clerk of an advocate under a banyan tree. We had no scope of meeting the advocate either. We would spend the entire day loitering around and eating puffed rice when hungry. We had no money to go to a restaurant. Whatever the clerk would say at the end of the day, my parents would listen. A peculiar thing about our bus travel was that to reduce the bus fare, we walked some distance on the road from the starting bus stand till we got tired. My father would stop the approaching bus after having walked a few kilometres. My father carried me on his shoulder while my younger sister would be in my mother's arms. My elder sister would walk painfully in between. When the children grew up and it became safer to live in the village, my father would travel to the town alone. He would return with no good news and frustration and despair would rule the atmosphere in our home.

My mother once asked me if I could become a collector. She believed I could help the common people if I did. However, she did not know how one became a collector, as she had never attended school. From time to time, she heard that I was doing well in my studies, and my teachers praised me when she met them in school occasionally. They even told her that I had the potential to become a collector one day.

I felt inspired by my mother and was driven to fulfil her wishes. Growing up in a less privileged society, I witnessed the sufferings of common people and it deeply affected me. It was painful to see poor and helpless individuals being mistreated and humiliated by others. I often saw tribal women come to our area to work in the agricultural fields, only to face harassment and mistreatment from conductors and other passengers on crowded buses. As a child, I would imagine being a collector and preventing such situations from occurring and punishing the wrongdoers. During Ganesh Puja and Saraswati Puja celebrations in primary and high schools, I would pray to god and goddess to make me a collector. However, I had no idea about the civil services examination.

After completing my tenth grade, I was searching for a good college to pursue further studies. However, my family's financial condition was not supportive enough to fund my education. I visited Ravenshaw College, Cuttack, to submit my application, as it was considered the best college in Odisha at that time. However, I found out that the monthly expense of staying in the hostel at Cuttack was more than double the cost of studying at Fakir Mohan College, Balasore. So I decided not to take admission to Ravenshaw College and believed that a student could achieve anything regardless of the college they study in. I moved to Balasore, which was not very far from my village, and started studying there. Whenever I had some free time, I loved to roam around the court premises, jail, and the banyan tree, where I used to come with my parents. I would recollect those bitter moments and get inspired to fulfil my mother's wishes.

I had a hard time paying the mess because I had to wait for the scholarship amount, which was disbursed towards the end of the year. I was not satisfied with the teaching in the college because of student elections and interference by the political parties. The college atmosphere was vitiated throughout those two years. All of my friends opted for private tuition, which I could not afford. I struggled harder and could not buy the books I needed. I borrowed some books from a laboratory assistant at the college who was referred to by a relative. The books were ten years old and the syllabus had been revised comprehensively by then. During this time, I met a clerk at the scholarship section of the college named Goswami babu. He was impressed by the marks I had secured in the matriculation examination and class tests. On learning about my financial condition, he assured me that he could disburse scholarships from two schemes of the government, although I was not sure if that was permissible. However, he kept some amount from my scholarship with him towards his share and would ask me to bring coconut and other things from the village. Despite this, I cannot forget his help.

I used to feel suffocated due to poverty at home so I decided to apply for a job. I would go to the market and buy the Employment News magazine to look for job openings. I was even willing to leave my studies if I could get any job, even that of a peon. However, I did not meet the minimum age requirement to apply for most jobs. Most of my classmates were from middle-class families and were very competitive. They were all preparing for entrance exams to become either doctors or engineers and attending private tuition or coaching classes. Unfortunately, I could not afford to do the same. Despite this, I did well in my college exams and participated in various events, earning recognition. All of this kept my motivation and morale high.

In the hostels where I lived during my college days, some of my seniors from the arts stream used to have discussions about the civil services examination. They would often boast about their abilities to clear the examination, feeling overconfident. However, I was aware that it was not an easy goal to achieve. Looking back, I realize that while many of those overconfident students did get placed well in life, they were unable to qualify for the civil services examination.

My immediate concern was to do something to get the family out of the trap of poverty. In childhood, I learned from my mother that my grandfather was a saint-like person. However, he died after complaining of abdominal pain at the age of hardly thirty years. He could not be administered any medicine. Her mother-in-law also died after suffering from the continued illness. The family had seen the unfortunate deaths of several children after birth. My father's brother, who became mad, could not be treated, and he died pathetically. I used to see both my parents falling sick several times on account of malnutrition and overwork in hazardous climates. I used to pray for their early recovery, as without them, our existence would not be possible. Each time my father's wealth worsened due to illness, I would feel the end of time for the entire family. There was no medical facility in the area.

As an intermediate goal, I aspired to become a doctor and began preparing for the entrance examination. Purna Chandra Das, one of my seniors who later became a successful doctor, was also preparing for the entrance exams, and I sought his guidance. My dream was to open a clinic in my village once I completed the course. I hoped to charge only a nominal fee from patients to help the poor and needy by becoming a doctor.

Towards the end of my second year in college, the advertisement for the engineering entrance examination was published. Initially, I was not interested as I was waiting for the medical entrance exam and did not know when it would take place. However, my friends were filling out the forms and asked me to apply as well. After our final board exams, we left the hostel and returned to our village. It was there that I received my admit card. With just one day to go until the engineering entrance test, I decided to return to the hostel to get a feel for the examination process. I had no intention of taking admission even if I qualified. Some of my old friends also came back to the hostel for the same purpose.

I was eagerly waiting for the notification of the state medical entrance examination. However, even after the results of the engineering entrance test were published, no notice had been released. I was not surprised to find my roll number in the newspaper in the list of successful candidates. The quality of teaching in our higher secondary classes was so poor that only three students from our reputed college received a call to take admission to the Regional Engineering College, Rourkela, the best engineering college in the state in the mid-1980s. I was confused and unsure if the medical entrance test would take place that year. If it did not take place, I would have no option for higher studies. My friends suggested that I take admission to the engineering college as studying engineering at Regional Engineering College, Rourkela, was like a dream to many. Additionally, if I qualified in the medical entrance later, I would still have the option of studying medical science after leaving the engineering college.

According to the notification received from the college, I was required to report and bring the necessary fees for my admission. However, it was difficult for me to arrange for the ₹1,000 needed. To collect the money, I sold my old bicycle that my mother had bought for me during high school. I received ₹300 from the sale and my mother also sold some of her jewellery. After much difficulty, we finally managed to gather the required funds. I travelled alone by train to Rourkela from Balasore. Fortunately, a clerk from our nearby village who worked at the college was able to help me. A part-time teacher from our high school gave me a letter to hand over to the clerk, requesting that he assist me after I arrived. The clerk advised me to meet another person from a nearby village in West Bengal who was involved in the vending business of betel leaves to various shops in Rourkela town.

One beautiful morning, I arrived at Rourkela station. After stepping out, I searched for the person who was described to me. I found him waiting for me with his bicycle. He greeted me with a very broad smile and a lot of affection, then made me sit on his bicycle and took me to his house in a slum near the railway lines of Rourkela town. The house was a kutcha structure with only one room on government land. He had stocked baskets of betel leaves which were received by train from the betel leaf-growing areas of West Bengal. I stayed in the slums and used all their facilities during my time in

Rourkela city. The house owner and his wife treated me very well and showed great affection. They even introduced me to their neighbours as their relative who had come to study at the Regional Engineering College, which made them very happy and proud. I felt extremely grateful for the love and warmth they showed me, which I had never experienced before. I stayed with them for a week until I was allotted a room in the hostel. Even after that, I would visit their family on some Sundays and spend quality time with them. I never complained about staying in their house in the slum as I felt comfortable and happy there.

After starting my classes, the notice for the medical entrance test was released. I felt helpless because when we were trying to gather the little money we needed for my engineering college admission, nobody came to our aid. My father approached a businessman who was also a villager to ask for a loan of ₹400, which we were short of. My father promised to repay the loan with interest through the sale of betel leaves from our betel leaf vine in the coming season. However, the man refused to help us, stating that no villager would benefit if I studied engineering. He was very close to us, and his refusal was very hurtful. We approached another distant relative, who was willing to give us money on the condition that I must marry his daughter after I finished my studies. This offer was not acceptable to our family, so we refused it. I was certain that it would be impossible to arrange any money once again for my medical college admission. With a heavy heart, I gave up on the idea of sitting for the medical entrance test. However, I made a strong resolution to study hard and excel in engineering.

I was informed that banks provide loans for education. I was confident that I could find a way to arrange the required funds. I did not share my financial difficulties with anyone in my college, not even my close friends, as I did not want to feel inferior in front of others. There were some underprivileged students in our college who received free meals in the mess. Such beneficiaries were often looked down upon by other students who were bearing their costs. Although I was eligible for a few scholarships, I decided to apply for an education loan of ₹10,000 at the State Bank of India's Jaleswar branch. Mr Ghosh, the branch manager, was a kind person who thoroughly examined my certificates and mark sheets. He contacted a schoolteacher from our locality, named Dhruba Charan Mandal, who agreed to serve as a guarantor for my loan. Mr Ghosh collected all of my documents and even visited my house in the village to verify my identity. He was convinced about my eligibility and believed that I would surely get a job after completing my studies and, thus, be able to repay the loan. After a few days, the loan was disbursed to me in several instalments. The loan amount was sufficient for me, taking into consideration my monthly expenses of about ₹300 for mess and other things. The loan amount was quite sufficient for me. Based on my performance in the first semester, I was granted a scholarship of ₹500 per month by Engineers India Ltd (EIL). I regularly received an amount of ₹3,000 every half year for four years. Another student at the college also received the same scholarship and I am grateful to EIL for their kind gesture. Thanks to the scholarship, I was more resourceful than many of my classmates. I was able to purchase a new bicycle and all the books and gadgets I needed, and I had no financial worries throughout my four years at Rourkela, allowing me to focus on my studies. I am grateful to god for his kindness, and once I started working, I was able to repay my bank loan with interest in a single instalment.

Although Rourkela is located in Odisha, it is a reflection of the pan-Indian culture. The steel plant is primarily responsible for creating a cosmopolitan and liberal culture in the area. When we attended the engineering college, it was the first time we had the opportunity to interact with students from other states. Approximately fifty per cent of the students were from Odisha, while the rest were from other states. We also had students from Nepal. Most of the Odia students struggled with conversing in either Hindi or English. Our interaction with non-Odia speaking students had an impact on our Hindi- and English-speaking skills. Generally, the students from outside Odisha were smarter and more fluent in English. Most of the students from Odisha attended government colleges and while they were very brilliant, they lacked in the area of smartness. However, when the internal examinations were held and the results of the first semester were out, it was proven that Odia students were far ahead of the other students. Despite their brilliance, most of the Odia students came from very humble backgrounds.

The syllabus and examination pattern that we used to follow during our time at Regional Engineering College, Rourkela, was very different from what is followed now. At that time, our college was under Sambalpur University, and our teachers did not even know who was setting the question papers. Despite this, they followed the syllabus thoroughly and referred to the best books. In my opinion, we had the best teachers during our time, who taught well, took class tests, conducted internal examinations, and were available to clear our doubts beyond class hours. Since the subject teacher did not set the question papers, we had to prepare extensively and deeply for the examinations. We made extra efforts to learn the subject by practising lessons from several books. The environment at Rourkela was very different from my previous college, Fakir Mohan College, Balasore. While the atmosphere in Balasore was very chaotic and undisciplined, the study environment at Rourkela was wonderful despite temporary disturbances due to the ragging of new students. Professor Somnath Mishra was an exemplary principal, who administered the college with distinction. In Balasore, the classrooms had faulty fans and tube lights, and the toilets had no water. These facilities were regularly damaged by the students, who also had a habit of breaking tables, chairs, and blackboards every day. Many of these students took private tuition and caused disturbances in the classroom for fun. Witnessing this, it was disheartening to see a lack of proper teaching, and it seemed like academic success was impossible in Balasore. In comparison, our college in Rourkela was a perfect setting for learning, with no disturbance in the classroom and hostel. During student elections, one could freely visit the library in the evening and walk around without any fear.

Achieving a score of seventy-five per cent in a semester was considered a remarkable accomplishment, known as obtaining honours, and those who did were given special treatment after the semester results were announced. The teachers would call out the names of these students, recognizing them by name and face. When I started college, a senior informed me about this prestigious achievement, and I became determined to obtain honours in all my exams. While my hostel mates would go out for dinner to town for birthday celebrations, movies, and other events, I would stay back in the hostel and study extra hours, similar to a few other students who were engrossed in their studies. The first semester was challenging, especially the engineering mechanics paper set by an IIT Kharagpur professor, which most students performed poorly on. One of the batchmates, Shubhankar Chatterjee, a very brilliant student, committed suicide after performing badly in the paper. We were all very shocked. Following his death, all students were given an opportunity for re-examination in the same paper. Fortunately, I was one of the very few students who received honours in the examination. This achievement filled me with immense joy and helped me regain my lost confidence. In the second semester, during a viva voce examination, one of my teachers Akshay Swain recognized my talent and predicted a bright future for me in front of my friends.

Four years passed very quickly. As a student, every day was full of events. Life felt like a never-ending race, whether in the classroom, playground, or workshop. One could not afford to let a single day pass without facing new challenges. The period was a crucial part of life, where one could develop selfless friends, nurture lifelong relationships, learn about competition, and test jealousy. I am grateful to have found friends who were genuinely happy for my achievements, even more than their own. At the end of eight semesters, I achieved my goal of securing an honours degree with first-class. This was a great source of satisfaction. My excellent scores in mathematics papers caught the attention of my teachers in the first four semesters.

The eighth semester was a crucial time for students at Regional Engineering College, Rourkela. Private companies were not visiting the campus frequently for employment opportunities. In those days, the public sector played a dominant role in the country. The central public sector companies conducted their recruitment tests. Like most engineering students at Regional Engineering College, Rourkela, I also desired to work at the Rourkela Steel Plant. After joining the plant, I wanted to devote my time to preparing for the civil services examination. However, I needed money to support my family back in the village. I received several job offers from public sector companies after writing the tests and facing interview boards. During an interview at the Steel Authority of India, I requested the chairman to post me at Rourkela when I was asked about my preference. Unfortunately, I was disillusioned when Steel Authority of India sent me to the Durgapur Steel Plant instead of Rourkela. My friends and seniors cautioned me about the unruly labour force at the Durgapur Steel Plant and dissuaded me from joining there.

Many students used to pursue higher studies after completing their undergraduate degree. Students who were better off financially, mostly from outside states, would write the GRE exam and seek admission for a Master's degree in US universities. Meanwhile, many bright students would take the CAT exam to qualify for admission to the Indian Institute of Management. However, I could not have considered those options because I had to arrange finance to study in IIMs, and there was no scholarship available. After spending four years in college for an engineering degree and going through great financial hardship, I could not think of going to a bank for an education loan again. The situation back at home demanded that I start earning. Although I had prepared for the common admission test for IIMs, I did not write the examination due to financial issues. As a good student, my only option was to sit for the GATE examination. In 1989, the Indian government announced a scholarship scheme to encourage and motivate talented students to pursue a master of technology (MTech) course. The scholarship amount was almost equal to the salary most Indian companies were offering to graduate engineers during that time. If a student scored well, they could study at either IIT or NITIE. Previously, the best graduates from Regional Engineering College, Rourkela, were taking the GATE examination. Students who scored more than 99 percentile were admitted to NITIE Mumbai. At least one student from Regional Engineering College, Rourkela, would invariably be admitted to NITIE Mumbai every year. Our teachers motivated us to pursue higher education. I scored well in the GATE examination and was accepted for admission to NITIE along with three of my friends. It was considered a prestigious achievement by everyone at the time. Therefore, I made the decision to move to Mumbai.

Several events occurred during the four years, but deep within me, the desire to become a collector remained alive. It was as if my mother repeatedly urging me towards it. I began to take an interest in reading newspapers and magazines and learning about current affairs to keep my desire alive. Debating and essay writing were my main areas of focus. Whenever I came to the village on holidays, my schoolteachers would remind me of my interest in civil services. My mother once said that becoming an engineer could earn me a good amount of money but it would be less useful to the disadvantaged people and society we lived in. Her own life experience reminded me that there were a large number of deprived and disadvantaged people who needed a sympathetic ear.

Those were the days when we did not have a telephone. Whenever I left to go to the town where I studied or to faraway places for a better life, I worried about my parents and their safety. When I returned home, they did not know where I had gone or if I was safe. They were unsure when they would see me next and always had me in their thoughts and prayers.

My mother used to walk behind me for a few furlongs outside of our village home, stopping only when I vanished out of her sight. Back then, it was an old world and not many thought of leaving for something better. However, my journey from the serpentine village road ended in the big city, and I covered thousands of miles on foot, rickshaw, bus, and train.

My parents would wait for me back in the village, constantly praying for my safety. At times, my mother's heartbeat would race and she would refuse to eat or drink until the postman arrived a week later with news that I had arrived safely and was doing well.

Unaware of what was happening in the village, I was determined to take responsibility on my slender shoulders since the age of sixteen to realize a dream and a secure future for my parents. Looking back today, I realize that I was never alone in my journey. My parents seemed to have walked alongside me, guiding me through their prayers and good wishes. Wherever I faltered, they led from the crossroads. All the milestones bear the marks of their pure love and promises.

8

The Collector's Mother

Upon completing our final exams and all necessary formalities at the engineering college, it was time to leave our hostel. I had to embark on my journey back to my village with all my belongings. My friends were leaving the college one by one, mostly by train from Rourkela railway station. There was a general feeling among us that we might not have the opportunity to meet most of our friends again. We were all busy noting each other's contact addresses and exchanging farewell messages. Since most of us did not have telephones, the agreement was to stay in touch through letters. While students were travelling to different destinations, some had jobs, others did not. A few had plans for higher studies but some did not reveal their plans. A large number of students were unsure of what the future held for them. As the excitement of returning home and family grew, the attachment to the four years we spent on campus began to feel less significant.

I stayed in the village for about a month and shared my future plans with my parents. I had informed them that I would take up a job as soon as I finished my studies at Rourkela.

However, I changed my plans and told them that I wanted to pursue higher studies for another two years. They had no objection to my decision. Until the 1990s, the village had no electricity, but it was full of greenery and thick forests. The tall trees provided shade, making it possible to walk at mid-day without feeling the heat of the sun. Every house had a garden with several horticulture species, such as coconut, guava, jackfruit, betel nut, palm trees, tropical fruits, and timber species. Being close to the sea, the breeze would be felt round the clock. One or two old friends would visit our house and we would spend leisurely time together in the familiar marketplaces. They had stopped studying after high school and were curious about my future plans. I was excited about my upcoming journey to Mumbai.

During our childhood, we used to receive visitors from Mumbai who held titles like Chourasia. They came to our village for business purposes. Farmers who grew betel leaves would dispatch their produce to Mumbai through intermediaries by trains. There were weekly markets held at different places in Bhograi. The farmers would bring and sell their betel leaves to the intermediaries there. The intermediaries-cum-aggregators would pack the leaves in bamboo baskets and send to the railway station by trucks. From there, the stock would be carried in goods bogies of passenger trains to Mumbai. After the traders in Mumbai received the stock, they would send currency notes by post through sealed insured letters. However, I am not sure if that was legally permissible. The farmers and intermediaries used to proudly open their insured letters in front of others, showing of the hundred rupee currency notes as a sign of their business success and superiority. The Chourasia would visit our village to learn about betel leaf vine and cultivation processes, and also to build mutual trust with the intermediaries as the whole business was based on informal relationships, credit, and correspondence. His two-in-one tape recorder was a unique gadget for the villagers, and Chourasia, clad in a white kurta and pajama, would happily roam around the village singing Hindi film songs and playing music from the recorder. The village children would flock around him, thinking of him as an alien, and sing '*Bombai se ayaamera dost*' in chorus. Although conversing with him in Hindi was difficult, there was no problem in understating each other. We would simply add '*hai*' and '*hun*' at the end of Odia sentences to make our Odia sound like Hindi.

Several years later, many young people from our area started travelling to Mumbai to engage primarily in the business of betel leaf. When these people visited the village from Mumbai, they would paint a rosy picture about the city. It was a dream for the children to visit Mumbai in their lifetime, to physically see the film stars. We were told that the film stars would be found moving around the city randomly, like the people in our village, whom we met almost daily. Anything connected to Mumbai after the film *Bobby* was very popular in our village. The boys who went to Mumbai would collect the betel leaf consignment arriving by train, unpack the bundles, sort the leaves once again, discard the rotten leaves, and go for vending to pan shops spread throughout the city. They did menial job in the city and would visit the village once or twice a year for long holidays. They loved to share tales about the city, particularly about the film stars but most of their versions were exaggerated and not based on facts. The villagers would gather around them, eager to know more about the big city. These young people were popularly called 'Mumbai Walas' and would show off their newfound status by wearing a lungi and a shirt with one button down from the neck, a gold chain around their neck, and chewing pan while wandering around. However, most of them would just loiter around and not do anything during their stay in the village. Some of them would get married and leave their wives behind. Such people would visit the village more frequently and stay for a longer period than the unmarried youths.

After receiving blessings from my parents, I embarked on my journey to Mumbai. I arrived at Victoria Terminus station on a beautiful morning and was greeted by my childhood friend Jagannath, who hailed from our neighbourhood. Jagannath and I shared a close bond during our childhood and would often engage in various games such as cricket, kabaddi, and cards. We used to play cricket and kabaddi with our village teams against teams from other villages. Despite the fact that his father caused us a lot of trouble for many years, Jagannath was always different. He found ways to befriend me during our school days, much to the displeasure of his father. Going to the cinema was our favourite pastime, and Jagannath would even steal dried coconuts from his house to sell at the market, so we could have enough money to buy two tickets to see movies regularly. Our village had four cinema halls within a radius of 3 to 4 kilometres. The cinema halls of the past were quite different from the modern ones we have today. They were made of mud walls, mud floorings, and roofing made of tin or straw. They had seating arrangements for three classes of visitors, totalling about a thousand. For me and my friend Jagannath, the place near the screen on a polythene sheet was good enough. Jagannath was attached to me and he would come to our house to study because of the environment in his own house. His father liked to gather people in the evenings to boast of his status. This disturbed Jagannath in his studies. He was good at studies and wanted to join the high school I was studying in after he passed out of the village primary school. He was two classes junior to me. However, his father disagreed and saw this as an opportunity to separate us. He sent Jagannath to a distant high school in Barbatia, which meant that he had to walk for more than 3 hours every day to travel to and from school, leaving him very tired by the evening. In addition, his father wanted him to work in the betel leaf vines, go to the market, and do other chores after and before school hours and during off days. He treated Jagannath very badly and used foul language. Despite his father's rough attitude, he remained my constant companion.

From my experience, I have found that one can remember lessons better in a quiet and more secluded place with no distractions. Once, we discovered an empty house of a wealthy man, which was used to guard his betel leaf vines and was a little distance away from our home. We obtained his permission to study there. In the evenings, we would go there together and stay overnight. Jagannath would cook and prepare simple food for us. In that isolated place, there was complete silence, which allowed me to concentrate better on my studies. As a result, I found that learning was easier, and my ability to retain the lessons I learned was much better. Jagannath was devastated when I left for Balasore to continue my studies after completing matriculation. He could not bear the constant abuse from his father. One day, he disappeared from the village just before his final high school examination. After a thorough search, he was found in Varanasi, working with a Marwari family in the betel leaf business. From there, he went to Mumbai and started his small betel leaf vending business for which he had acquired the necessary skills. He was content with his income and life.

Jagannath was very pleased to welcome me at the railway station. We went to his place in Gol Dewal, a crowded business area in south Mumbai. His small room housed his personal belongings and betel leave stock. During the day, he would travel by local train, on foot, or by taxi to deliver betel leaves to various places. In the afternoon, he would return to his room to collect fresh stock from an intermediary, sort the leaves according to customers, and prepare for the next day's deliveries. He would work until late in the evening before resting. After a long day, I noticed that the men in the area would sleep on the road outside their houses, blocking the entry of vehicles with hand rickshaws and other barriers. The area had no mosquitoes, but it was challenging for people to huddle together in small rooms during rainy nights. My experience was not very pleasant. Many young people from rural areas were drawn to Mumbai by the promise of fulfilling their dreams. However, it seems that these dreams faded for many of them. Despite being able to earn some money and support their families back in their hometowns, their lives was very difficult. They did not have proper toilets facilities, bathing areas, kitchen spaces, and places to rest. They were forced to live in overcrowded rooms that had high rent. As a result, most of them could not bring their families and were forced to remain apart from their loved ones.

I was introduced to the local train and public transportation system in the city and with Jagannath's help reached the National Institute of Industrial Engineering (NITIE) for my admission process. Fortunately, I was allotted a hostel room immediately. I visited Jagannath quite regularly, and he would also come to my hostel. He was very happy to have me in his city.

NITIE Mumbai is located in one of the most beautiful areas of the city, surrounded by Vihar Lake and Powai Lake. Before the 1992 Mumbai bomb blast, the situation was different, and there were fewer security restrictions. Vihar Lake is a crucial source of drinking water for the city, along with a few other sources. Despite this, the visitors were allowed to enter the lake area. On Sundays and holidays, massive crowds of people and children would come to play games for a fee.

Boating was not permitted. We could walk from our institute campus along the banks of the lake and reach the film city at Goregaon to see the outdoor shooting of films and series.

NITIE was a unique institution when compared to Regional Engineering College, Rourkela. All the fifty students who took admission in the postgraduate diploma in industrial engineering (PGDIE) course were toppers in their batches in IITs and other engineering colleges. They were considered for admission after scoring a minimum of 99 percentile in the GATE examination. Ten other candidates who took admission were industry sponsored. Except for four of us from Regional Engineering College, Rourkela, the rest were from different states of the country. The faculty members were highly experienced, and most of them had industry exposure. Being in NITIE instilled a sense of pride and excitement in us.

According to a notification from the Government of India, the PGDIE course was considered equivalent to an MTech course, making students eligible for a monthly stipend of ₹1,800. The stipend is a major draw for students from middle-class families. The degree from NITIE was considered equivalent to that of IIMs' in terms of recruitment prospects. NITIE offers world-class facilities such as a mess, hostel accommodation, classrooms, a library, an auditorium, and a green campus. The institute truly cares for its students. The course duration is eighteen months, including a six-month industry attachment to provide practical experience in solving real-life problems under the guidance of faculty members. During the industry attachment, students receive stipends from the companies, including food and other facilities. NITIE has a reputation for offering good placement opportunities in the corporate sector, including multinationals. Admission to NITIE is highly competitive, and it is considered an excellent alternative to the IIMs for those who cannot attend due to financial or other reasons. Only engineers were eligible for admission and the course is a blend of engineering and management. Established in 1963 with assistance from the International Labour Organization of the United Nations, NITIE was created to provide a pool of trained industrial engineering professionals for the country. While the postgraduate programme is the institute's flagship programme, it also conducts short-term training programmes, research, and consultancy work. The institute follows a quarterly system, which differs from the semester system used in other institutes. This system keeps students under tremendous pressure, with two internal examinations and a quarter-ending examination every quarter, along with several classroom presentations. However, the students adapt to the pressure and are well-prepared for the corporate sector. NITIE is well-recognized in Mumbai for its contribution.

The coursework at NITIE was highly demanding, leaving little room for extracurricular activities. Despite this, some of our seniors were quietly preparing for the civil services examination. In the past, a few bright students had successfully qualified for services such as IAS, IFS, or IPS. Most of the students were toppers in their respective engineering colleges, making it easy for those who were interested in Indian Engineering Services to secure the coveted government jobs. Some of my batchmates also began preparing for the examination, but overconfidence was common among the NITIE students.

The pattern of the civil services examination followed during those days was changed later. To qualify for the preliminary examination, we had to write two papers. The general knowledge paper was compulsory and the second paper was to be chosen from a list of subjects. I chose mechanical engineering as my optional subject, as I had studied the course thoroughly and was feeling confident. Since my childhood days, I had been participating in quizzes and general knowledge competitions. I secured a good rank in the engineering services examination, which led to a job offer in the Indian Railways Services of Mechanical Engineers. I had performed exceedingly well in various recruitment tests for public sector companies and the GATE examination. Hence, I thought that clearing the first stage would be quite easy. In each of my attempts for the civil services examination, crossing the first hurdle was never an issue.

NITIE provided us with the necessary skills to be problem solvers in the corporate sector. We were exposed to a diverse range of subjects including core industrial engineering topics, which helped us improve our analytical and communication skills, and gave us an expansive knowledge base. Towards the end of our course at NITIE, several companies visited the campus for placement purposes. The students dressed formally and participated in interviews. The best companies were slotted for the initial day, while public sector units came towards the end. Ideally, the students wanted jobs in companies known for good career prospects, salary, and other perks. All the students got jobs in the corporate sector, with some not-so-bright students getting picked up by public sector companies at the end.

A few days before the placement interviews, I came across an advertisement for a special recruitment for the post of lecturer in industrial engineering at NITIE. I applied for the job casually but to my surprise, I was called for an interview. During the interview, the director offered me the job on the spot. Many faculty members at NITIE were alumni of the institute and there was no better candidate to teach industrial engineering than someone from NITIE. Despite the fact that teaching did not seem to attract the brightest of students, I was drawn to the job because of the good salary and the fact that it would give me sufficient time to prepare for the civil services examination. I did not want to sit for the campus placement because I was determined to prepare for the civil services examination. One of my batchmates, who was also preparing for the exam and going to join the Indian Railways, suggested that I opt for the lectureship as it would provide me with the best environment and enough time to prepare for the exam.

After completing my course, I left for my village, where I spent fifteen days contemplating my options, threats, and opportunities. I then returned to join as a lecturer. Everyone who knew me from the past two years at the institute was welcoming and supportive of my return. I was given an office room on the floor and I met with all the professors I knew, who expressed their satisfaction with my joining and gave me several pieces of advice. I was provided with single-room accommodation in a hostel by the lakeside, which was a six-storied building. Most of the time, I stayed alone there until I moved to a type four apartment on campus.

Initially, I was not assigned any teaching job for the postgraduate classes, although I was coordinating the industry projects of the students. Later, I was made a co-course coordinator for a few courses for executives from the industries for a short-term duration of one to two weeks and was assigned to take some classes. As a course coordinator, I was solely responsible for the outcome of the courses. Soon, my favourite teacher, Professor Thomas Mathew took over as the director of the institute, and he took care of me like his son. Professor Mathew would include me in various consultancy teams. The institute received offers for consultancy services from various companies to solve their problems for which the director would constitute expert teams by drawing professors from relevant disciplines. Sixty per cent of the earned amount from a consultancy assignment would be shared by the team members while the remaining 40 per cent would go to the institute's fund. I got exposure to many industries and travelled widely throughout the country with other senior professors in this connection. I was required to stay back with other junior members of the team to take some readings and observations in the field and provide them to the senior members to help in analysis and formulate recommendations and make presentations to the top company officials. Professor Mathew would ask me to join the senior professors to go to other cities like Pune, Nasik, Kolkata, Bangalore, Raichur, and Dispur to conduct short-term courses. However, some senior faculty members became jealous of me due to the open patronage and support from Professor Mathew.

I supported my parents financially while I was studying at NITIE. I sent more than half of my scholarship to them, as they needed it. They were instructed not to do any labour work for wages, as the money I sent was enough for their needs. After I got my first job, I earned a good amount of money and continued to support my family. I transferred all my income to my father, who used it to rebuild his life by putting some money into agriculture and building a new house. Professor Mathew never knew about my personal problems but still supported me in every way possible. He believed in my potential and would always praise me in front of others. No one dared to do anything against me because of his support.

My main reason for staying at NITIE and working there was to prepare for the civil services examination. However, I soon realized that Mumbai did not have a conducive environment for civil services preparation. Unlike Delhi, there was not much enthusiasm or awareness about the Indian Administrative Service. Even after the final results were published, very few newspapers in Mumbai reflected the concerns of the intelligentsia. They would only discuss why not many candidates from Maharashtra were getting into civil services, resulting in a greater number of outsiders taking up positions in the state's bureaucracy. People in Maharashtra take great pride in their children holding powerful positions, but the average person there is unaware of services like IAS, IPS, and IFS. Due to the salary and perks, there was general disinterest in government jobs. People in Mumbai were content with their city life and had no desire to venture out to rural areas in remote parts of the country for employment. Mumbai's business sector dominated the economic environment, unlike in underdeveloped regions of the country. The children were not interested in making multiple attempts and studying hard for jobs that did not offer significant benefits. City dwellers aimed to earn a good amount of money, which they found easily by working in private companies or engaging in business. During my time at the campus, I rarely encountered any other individual who aspired to work in the services sector, although a few students at the institute were preparing for it. One of our seniors had made it into the Indian Administrative Service, but instead of joining, he left for the USA to pursue higher studies at Oklahoma State University.

I purchased all the necessary books and subscribed to important magazines such as *Yojana*, *Kurukshetra*, *Mainstream*, *Competition Success Review*, and *Civil Services Review*. To appear for the mains examination, I had to select two subjects. My old friends living in other cities suggested that I choose physics and mathematics as they were high-scoring. These subjects were quite tough, but the toppers from IITs had also chosen these subject combinations. My friends even advised me to drop mechanical engineering as it was not scoring. Only a few engineering students were opting for engineering subjects, just like the medical students who were not taking medical science as a subject.

I regretted not listening to my friends when I chose my subjects. My friend opted for physics and mathematics and got accepted. I, on the other hand, thought all subjects were equal and believed that hard work would lead to success. I chose sociology as my second subject and bought all the necessary books recommended by top students and coaching institutes. I studied diligently and memorized everything, but I later realized that I had not practised enough writing and did not seek help from coaching institutes. I learned that writing good answers in a subject like sociology requires special skills and practice.

I took the mains examination from 1991 to 1994 with mechanical engineering and sociology as my subject combination. When the results were announced, I rushed to the Churchgate Railway Station and walked up to the Press Information Bureau office nearby to search for my roll number from top to bottom and from bottom to top. If I found my roll number missing, I would feel miserable, as if the earth beneath my feet was crumbling. After spending a few hours searching, I would return to my room alone at midnight. To calm myself down, I would sit under the shower for hours to cool down. I would then make a fresh resolution not to let this happen again and start preparing from the next day onwards.

I had travelled the paths of my life alone. There was no one to enquire about my successes, failures, achievements, and results. My parents were generally not aware of what I was doing. On campus, no one was bothered about the civil services and me. Whenever I would come to my village during holidays, some teachers would inquire about my general well-being and if I was still thinking of becoming an IAS officer. However, some of them would look down upon me as I took up a teaching job and would avoid meeting me.

I had a colleague named Philip, who also joined NITIE as a lecturer. He had studied with us as an industry-sponsored candidate. Being senior to us, he was already married and had two lovely kids. His wife Zita was a good housewife who took up a job subsequently. My friend would invite me over to his house for food, and we would play badminton on the campus. He and his wife knew what I was doing on campus and provided me with great company. On holidays, he would invite me to join his trips to nearby places in Mumbai, like Matheran, where we would have a good time. His wife was very good at cooking fish curry in South Indian style. I would have a good time playing with their children. Zita would enquire about my personal issues like health and provide help if needed. She always felt that I would qualify for the services and would motivate me. I had a classmate named Buddhadeb who was also a faculty member. He had joined as a lecturer before me. Although he wanted to appear for the civil services, he found the examination too complex and difficult, so he focused on teaching and research instead. Both my classmates and their families provided me with mental support and physical comfort whenever I needed them. I will always be grateful to them.

Visiting my village regularly from Mumbai was very important to keep my parents happy. I always kept any negative news related to me from them and only communicated harmless and positive developments. Whenever there was a long holiday, I would book my train ticket up to Kharagpur, which took more than 40 hours. After taking my luggage from the train, I would take a rickshaw to the nearby bus stand. From there, I would take a bus to reach the Digha border in West Bengal, which took about 4 hours. Once I reached the Digha border, I would take another rickshaw to a bus stand in Chandaneswar. The last leg of my journey was a few kilometres by bus. After getting off the bus in Jal Soharia, I would carry my luggage on my shoulder or in my hand. I used to walk to my village along a long and winding road, which would take me over an hour. The entire journey was exhausting, spanning over two days. I never informed my parents about my date of arrival beforehand, and every time it was a surprise. I did it intentionally because if, for some reason, I could not reach the scheduled date and time, my mother would become anxious and her health would deteriorate. Since there was no means to communicate in case of a delay or any other sudden development, I thought it was better to arrive home without any prior intimation to save her from health issues. They got used to my way, but they would expect me to arrive during festivals. The happiness that I saw in my family on my arrival will always remain etched in my memory. I used to wake my parents up at late hours of the night. My mother would welcome me with a loud cry of joy, hugging me by calling my name. Soon, my father would light a lantern and clear the clutter from the verandah to make space for us. He would take out the fishing net and get ready to catch fish from our pond. The fire in the hearth would be lit and my mother would start cooking rice and fish curry. Under the lantern light fuelled by kerosene, I would sit beside them and share my experiences and catch up on the happenings since my last visit. Finally, very late in the night, I would go to sleep, feeling relieved of all my stress and strain within minutes. For me, there was no other place on earth than home. Whenever I had self-doubt or lacked focus, visiting home would recharge me with energy and purpose. However, leaving home to return to Mumbai always left me with a heavy heart. I would assure my parents that I would be back soon. My parents eagerly waited for news of my safe arrival and well-being. They would visit the post office in the neighbouring village several times in the following weeks and would only be satisfied after reading my letter, confirming that all was well.

I persevered with my efforts for the civil services examination. Unfortunately, on my first attempt, I scored poorly in my optional subjects during the mains examination.

I was determined to give it my all and improve. However, I was unsure why I had received such low marks. My friends informed me that the UPSC followed a process of normalization. This meant that an unannounced procedure was used to ensure that candidates from all subjects were treated equally. For instance, while it was possible to score a perfect 600 out of 600 marks in mathematics, the same was not possible for arts subjects. If the actual marks scored were not treated as per a specific formula, only students from high-scoring subjects like mathematics would qualify, putting science students above the others. Thus, the marks awarded to a candidate could be different from what he or she actually scored. I received my marks for the optional subjects and found that I had not made much improvement in sociology, which worried me as it could have a negative impact on my overall result. Although I had prepared well, I received average marks in both papers on mechanical engineering, which left me confused as to why my scores were low in my favourite subject. I attributed this to the UPSC's process of moderating scores for individual subjects, which made it difficult to compare candidates with varied subject choices. However, I was performing well in general studies and essay writing. Despite this, I was lost and confused about my next steps.

Some students from my junior batches at NITIE were also preparing for the examination. They would come to me seeking guidance and were surprised by my level of preparation. However, when three of them cleared the exam and I did not, everyone was very surprised.

When I was excelling in my studies and achieving many other things, I decided to take the civil services examination. I did not consider any alternative career options because I was confident I would succeed. While studying at NITIE, my friends were applying for gas and telephone connections because there used to be a long waiting period to obtain these facilities. However, I did not bother to apply because I believed that these facilities would be easily available to me once I became a civil servant. I was not interested in a teaching job, which I landed in incidentally, nor did I pursue another career option in the Indian Engineering Service. After three unsuccessful attempts, I began to think that the entire civil services examination system was too complex, like a game of gambling. I questioned how the best student in engineering could be compared to someone who chose literature. The best engineering or medical student was not even taking their own subject but instead choosing from subjects they had not studied at the undergraduate level. This left me feeling despair, and I feared that I would not be able to fulfil the promise I made to my mother to become a collector. I examined the statistics of the number of candidates taking the examination compared to the vacancies and the demand for increasing the number of attempts. There were even examples of unsuccessful candidates attempting suicide after exhausting their attempts.

All my classmates had already secured good jobs in the corporate sector by then. Some of them even had left for the USA and were earning a good salary. Whenever any of my friends were in Mumbai, they would visit me at NITIE and stay with me for a few days. Some of them even brought me electronic gadgets as gifts, which were not available in India. I had three friends, Karanjit Singh, Jagannath Das, and Shailesh Dubey, who were working in Mumbai. They would often visit me on weekends, and we would go out to our favourite restaurant in Saki Naka. Although all of them had considered taking the same examination at some point, due to personal reasons, they dropped the idea. However, my friends always encouraged and motivated me towards my goal whenever we met. Without their company, I would have felt quite lonely in such a big city

Although I may have appeared frail, I was a strong person from within, with a positive inclination to do good for society. When observing social disparity, I often questioned the existence of God. As a child, I would go with my mother to the Chandaneswar Temple, but I would refuse to enter and instead wait outside. I would ask my mother why people like us, who were good but poor, had to suffer while others lived better lives. Although she would take me to temples, she never answered my question. I refused to visit any astrologer or temple for a long time as a form of protest against the inequalities and inequities in society.

One day, while reading the *Times of India*, I came across a news article about an astrologer who claimed to have predicted the assassination of our late prime minister Shri Rajiv Gandhi. This astrologer became famous after the tragic incident. According to the article, he was available for consultation at the Hotel Ambassador, but only by prior appointment and for a fee. Despite feeling agitated, I decided to consult him. I arrived at the hotel on a sunny afternoon and inquired about him. I understood that the person in question was seated in front of a market close to the famous Eros cinema hall. After making some inquiries, I approached him for a consultation. He charged five times the amount for a full prediction compared to one question, so I paid for one question only. My question was whether I could become an IAS officer. The astrologer carefully examined my palm for some time and then told me bluntly that I was not likely to get the job. Instead, he said that my destiny was in business, where I would be highly successful and become a wealthy man. He also predicted that I would pass away in a foreign country, far from my place of birth. I felt disgusted and quickly withdrew my hand, disagreeing with him. I replied firmly that astrology was nothing less than a fraud. I even argued that no one could stop me from becoming an IAS officer. The astrologer was a kind-hearted and wise man who asked me to sit and cool down. While trying to pacify me, he stated that his prediction was based on the lines on my palm. He further stated that if someone had strong willpower, they could change their destiny and that the lines on the palm were not important for such people. He said he knew many such examples. According to him, God would always fulfil the wish of a strong-willed person. My encounter with the astrologer had a very deep impact on me and I returned to my residence thereafter.

I had a classmate named Satyabarata who worked at the Bhilai Steel Plant. He was a brilliant student and had been a topper throughout his career. He was also preparing for the civil examination with a subject combination of mathematics and mechanical engineering. Unfortunately, he could not clear the exam. Both of us were inclined to continue with engineering subject because we had proven our merit in it. It was difficult to find time to study a subject like physics extensively. Satyabarata and I were very friendly and close, so every time I travelled to my village from Mumbai, I would break my journey at Bhilai and stay with him for a few days. We would then travel together to Odisha on the train. My friend and I would travel to our respective destinations in Kharagpur and Bhubaneswar, and we synchronized our return trips to travel together for a part of the journey to our workplaces. We cherished our time together and had a strong bond. My friend had ordered study materials from a coaching institute and recommended that I change my optional subject. After reviewing the syllabus, I replaced sociology with mathematics since changing two subjects would have been too difficult. The coaching centre's materials on mathematics helped me prepare. Unfortunately, neither of us had the guidance of a successful candidate or a good teacher, but the environment for preparation in Bhilai was just as good as in Mumbai.

In Mumbai, I was living alone and unsure if I was making progress in the right direction. Getting food was a challenge every day. My parents visited me for a few days during this time, which was a relief. However, the aftermath of the bomb blast in Mumbai in 1992 was terrifying. Many people, mostly labourers, were leaving the city in crowded trains out of fear for their lives. There were reports of innocent people being brutally attacked on the streets. To stay safe, many people remained confined to their homes. The police, under significant stress, was exhibiting aggressive behaviour and would even beat up people for minor traffic violations or offences. From the top of my hostel building, I could see many localities and slums burning here and there. Movement was restricted, and I was confined to the campus. Fortunately, there was no need to leave the institute. One of our friends was working in a private company located near Dalal Street. He was present at the Mumbai Stock Exchange on the fateful day when a series of bomb blasts shook the city. He died on the spot due to the shock and after-effects of a nearby explosion. Coincidentally, he had visited my place a few days before. While having tea and sitting on our usual culvert in front of the hostel, I had a look at his palm lines. I told him that his lifeline was incomplete and asked if he had shown it to any astrologer before. He replied sadly that there was a bad prediction about his life, for which his parents had been taking extra care from his childhood. For this reason, he was not allowed to go to the USA for higher studies, even though he was a topper in his class at IIT Kharagpur. I closed the topic by stating that astrology was a joke and nothing should be taken seriously. However, after hearing the news of my friend's death, I could not help but relate it to the astrological prediction and felt deeply worried.

I was worried that my parents would hear about the unrest and developments in Mumbai and become very upset. To reassure them, I sent a telegram home with a single line saying that I was safe in Mumbai. However, upon receiving the message, they started interpreting it in their own way, arguing that if everything was fine, there was no need for me to send a telegram. The villagers also agreed with them. Upset by this, they packed their luggage and travelled from Kharagpur station to Mumbai in an ordinary class train, despite not knowing how to reach me beyond my postal address. Additionally, they did not know how to communicate with fellow passengers since they did not know Hindi. Once they arrived at VT station in Mumbai, a co-passenger helped them find where Jagannath was staying. I received a phone call from Jagannath informing me about the arrival of my parents. They were happy to hear that everything was fine at my end. With the help of Jagannath, they were able to locate my hostel. Although I was surprised to see them at my hostel, I was also a little irritated. The reason for my irritation was the fact that if anything had happened to them while travelling, the damages could have been severe. They had to travel in a train for two days and did not know the language of the people they were travelling with, could not communicate with anyone, could not read the names of stations, and did not know where to get off. However, their pure love brought them to the city. Soon after, I was allotted an apartment on campus, and we had a great time there. My mother set up a kitchen and cooked food using a kerosene-fueled stove. This was the only time my parents visited and stayed with me since I left my village after finishing my matriculation exams. I felt very blessed in their presence. I was occupied with official work for at least fifteen days every month. I have been assigned the task of teaching quality engineering to management students, which requires my complete dedication. My area of expertise lies in a subject called 'Taguchi Technique for Quality Engineering', which demands a strong understanding of statistics. To prepare for this subject, I had to delve deep into statistics, which proved to be extremely beneficial in the future.

Though I wanted to devote full time to my preparation, I could not afford to leave my job as my family needed financial support to survive. Looking at my plight, my friend in Bhilai suggested I take a leave of absence for a few months so that we could prepare together for the upcoming examination. He offered to provide me with food and accommodation while I stayed with him. Convinced that this was a good idea, I approached Dr Thomas Mathew and requested a four-month leave of absence. He granted my request and assured me not to worry about anything. I then left for Bhilai with my books and reading materials and entrusted the keys to my flat to my friend Buddhadeb, who was staying there with his family. I found the best possible place to study at Bhilai. My best friend had a cook and made arrangements for me to stay in his house.

As nobody else was staying in the house, I had absolutely no distractions. I had a full twenty-four hours at my disposal every day. My friend used to go to work at the steel plant and would come back in the evening. He would join me in studying after returning. Since I had no other commitments, I could study for about eighteen hours a day. I would only go out for less than an hour to the nearby market to get some fresh air. Although my friend was a topper in our engineering college with an excellent memory, I requested him to take leave and devote more time to studying. Unfortunately, he could not take a long leave and could not devote full hours to preparation. We both wanted to qualify together for the civil services.

A few days before the exam, my friend and I travelled by bus to stay with his family near the Lingaraj Temple in Bhubaneswar. They took good care of us as we prepared for our exams. We sat for the mains examination at Ravenshaw College in Odisha. As each paper ended, I felt good about my performance. I answered all the questions in both mathematics papers, and I was confident that all my answers were correct. I also did well in papers for mechanical engineering, mathematics, English essay, and general studies papers. I knew that UPSC would moderate the marks, but I still had a positive feeling that I would qualify. While I was not sure how many marks I would get, I was optimistic about my performance. This was 1994, and I cleared the exam.

I felt quite jubilant and decided to visit my village to spend a few days with my parents. After my visit, I returned to

Mumbai and reported to Professor Mathew. I devoted my time to teaching at the institute, working on consultancy assignments with seniors, and conducting in-house training programmes for some companies. On 26 June 1994, the preliminary examination for the year 1994 was conducted, and a total of 283,189 candidates applied for it. I selected the Maharashtra Public Service Commission building in Mazgaon as my centre for the examination. After the preliminary examination, UPSC shortlisted 11,857 candidates for the mains examination. The mains (written) examination was conducted from 16 December 1994 to 16 January 1995 and 10,548 candidates appeared for it. I was fortunate to have my centre at Ravenshaw College, Cuttack.

I was eagerly waiting for the results of the written examination. As soon as the announcement was made, I rushed to the Press Information Bureau office to learn about my qualification for the viva voce. A total of 1,456 candidates had qualified for the personality test, which began in New Delhi on 17 May 1995. Since UPSC does not reveal the marks secured by the candidates before the viva voce, it was impossible to know one's relative position based on the written examination alone. The number of candidates called for interviews was double the number of vacancies. It was important to secure good marks in the written examination as well as perform well in the viva voce. I was very confident that I had done well in both and focused on reading current affairs and reviewing the syllabus. I was hopeful that I would make it to the final list. My experience in teaching, consulting, and research boosted my morale. Although I was scheduled to appear before the interview board, I did not take any mock tests.

I travelled to Delhi on the Rajdhani Express and stayed at the home of an army doctor named Deepak, the brother of a friend of mine. Before my personality test, an Indian Revenue Services officer advised me to remain calm and appear natural without any preparation. I followed his advice and wore formal attire consisting of pants, a shirt, and a tie. I then appeared before a panel chaired by Shri S J S Chatwal, who was known for being very tough.

I felt that my interview went well. The interviewers were very cordial. However, I could not answer a few questions related to my home state of Odisha, as I was not very familiar with its geography, culture, and political developments. The reason for this difficulty was that I had not lived in Odisha for the last few years. I come from a remote village on the border of the state, far away from politically sensitive places like Bhubaneswar and Cuttack. Nevertheless, I was able to answer questions related to my work experience in management, engineering, teaching, consultancy, and research. Overall, I was satisfied. While I saw the candidates discussing their performance in the interviews with their own groups and family members outside the UPSC building, I had no one to discuss with, so I left and I boarded the Rajdhani Express the next day for Mumbai. However, my reservation was not confirmed, and it was an RAC ticket. The ticket collector pushed me down as soon as the train moved. I contacted my friend Rajeev, who worked as a consultant, and requested him to book an air ticket for me. With his help, I was able to return to Mumbai in the evening.

I experienced a lot of tension before the exam results were announced. I had not considered any other career option, so failing the exam would have been disastrous. I received encouragement from my close colleagues and associates who believed in miracles. I had been preparing for the exam for several years and had become so obsessed with becoming a civil servant that I could not see any other good opportunities beyond that goal. Although I was not unhappy with my job as a lecturer at NITIE, teaching was not my career of choice, and I had hoped to leave soon. However, to continue teaching at NITIE, I would need to complete a PhD programme, for which I had registered for a fellowship programme but did not pursue. All my pride in being an achiever and a good student seemed meaningless in the face of my failure. While my friends were getting settled down, getting married, and leaving for better prospects abroad, I was becoming increasingly lonely. Worst of all, I feared not being able to face my parents and others in the village who believed I would become an IAS officer. How could I not keep my word? The fear of not achieving success in the examination had gone deep into my psyche. Even today, after so many years, I wake up in the night from nightmares of not getting into the coveted service.

On 23 June 1995, the results of the civil services examination of 1994 were declared. As soon as I heard the news about the announcement of the final result on television, I hurried to the Press Information Bureau office located near the Churchgate Station, carrying with me a bag full of hope, anxiety, and stress. There were only a few people present, who were quietly checking the list. I did not see any celebration around. Most of the candidates and people were quiet. As per the announcement, 705 candidates were recommended for various services. Mr Ashutosh Jindal had topped the list that year. With the hope of success, I started searching for my name from the bottom of the list pasted on the wall. As I was going through the list, I felt nervous and hopeless. I could not find my name and started to worry. Suddenly, I burst into great joy when I saw my name and roll number on the second page. I had wanted this so badly and it felt unbelievable to see it in writing. Although I knew there could not have been another person with my name, I double-checked my roll number just to be sure. I was certain that I had made it to the list that I had been eagerly waiting for since my childhood. I could not hold back my tears of joy and felt a great sensation of warmth all over my body like never before. I looked up at the clear blue sky over the Arabian Sea and thanked God for that day. It was a long pause filled with gratitude and excitement.

The first thing I wanted to do after my success was to let my mother know about the news of my success. Unfortunately, no one in our village had a telephone, so communication had to be done through postal letters. However, one of my school friends who had dropped out of school had started a fertilizer retail shop at a bus stand in the village of Chowki. He had managed to get a telephone connection despite the difficulties. To communicate more effectively, I suggested to my mother that she come to his shop at a fixed time twice a week, on Mondays and Fridays. If there was ever an urgent message to be communicated, I would ask Aniruddha to send his brother on his bicycle to convey the message to my parents in the village. I went to a nearby telephone booth and dialled my friend's number. I asked him to inform my mother that I had passed the civil services examination and would become a collector. My friend spread the news quickly throughout the area, bringing great joy to my parents.

Over the next two months, I celebrated with my close friends and colleagues in Mumbai. On the same day, my dear friends Karanjit, Jagannath Das, Shailesh Dubey, and Buddhadeb joined in the festivities. I received congratulatory messages from Professor Mathew and all the faculty members I was associated with as a student and as a faculty member. We celebrated with Philip, his wife Zita, and their family with much happiness.

I visited my village after breaking my return journey from Dibrugarh, where I had been for official work. For the first time, I did not bring lots of books with me. My mother welcomed me like a victorious emperor. My father was also extremely happy but would not express it much. By then, people in our area started addressing my mother as collector's mother, a name which she kept until her last breath. My schoolteachers, especially Ishwar Chandra Giri, the headmaster, were the happiest of all. His prediction of me becoming an IAS officer, which he made during my school days, had come true. He took pride in publicly stating it and organized a function in the school for my felicitation. The teachers shared my lifelong struggle and the hardships my parents had gone through with the students. I also met a journalist who interviewed and featured me in the Odia newspapers. The news had already been spread around the nearby villages that for the first time, someone from their area had become an IAS officer, that too from a very disadvantaged family.

Although the hostile elements in the village were no longer causing us harm, we had become quite insignificant due to various developments in the 1980s. However, our struggle for survival had given us a lot of resilience. Now, new hopes had dawned upon us. We would no longer be targeted and falsely implicated. No one could take away our dignity anymore. The people who had tortured my parents for decades were now silent. They neither came to our house nor expressed any feelings after hearing about my success. Many well-known people in the locality visited our home and expressed their happiness. From that day forward, all the fear for life that my parents had from the inimical elements simply disappeared.

However, the scars left on our bodies because of the various attacks still remind us of the days of horrors our family had to endure. In one such attack, we had to run out of the house in the middle of the night. The house was left open, and the rice being cooked in the kitchen burned. Someone poisoned our pond, killing all the fish in it. We feared drinking water from the tube, lest somebody had poisoned it as well. We had received open threats to leave the village. My mother was attacked, and so was my father in the night while he was on his way back home from the market. A plot was hatched to kill him by drowning in the pond. Radhakrishna Pal and his family cheated us. They tied my parents and dragged them because they protested against Pal and his family cheating us. There was betrayal. There was injustice. In the village, no one heard our cries, and no one gave us shelter. They remained mute spectators to our sufferings.

However, we survived and overcame all the obstacles because of God's kindness.

About the Author

Bishnupada Sethi is an IAS officer of the 1995 batch. Currently, he is the principal secretary to the Odisha government. He has served in one of most backward regions of the country such as Kandhamal, Gajapati, Sonepur, Nuapada and Rayagada. His role in improving the lives of people in the region earned him much appreciation from the National Human Rights Commission.

Bishnupada is a recipient of distinguished alumnus awards from National Institute of Technology, Rourkela, and National Institute of Industrial Engineering (now IIM), Mumbai. He was awarded the President of India Silver Medal for his contribution to Census 2011. Sethi's performance as a special relief commissioner during the 2019 super cyclone Fani was recognized as an exemplary model throughout the world, including by the United Nations. He is also the recipient of the Bhima Bhoi Award for his contribution to popularizing Mahima philosophy.

He is a published author and writes articles for various publications. His books on poetry, namely *Where Shall I go, My World of Words, Beyond Feelings* and *Beyond Here and Other Poems,* have been received well and translated into multiple languages. Sarala Sahitya Sansad felicitated him for his contribution to mystic poetry.

About the Author